Frederick G. Shinn

Musical Memory and its Cultivation

Frederick G. Shinn

Musical Memory and its Cultivation

ISBN/EAN: 9783744778244

Printed in Europe, USA, Canada, Australia, Japan

Cover: Foto ©ninafisch / pixelio.de

More available books at **www.hansebooks.com**

TO

SIR WALTER PARRATT,

MASTER OF THE MUSIC AND PRIVATE ORGANIST TO THE QUEEN,

WHO, IN HIS CAPACITY OF DIRECTOR OF THE MUSIC AND DICTATION CLASSES AT THE ROYAL COLLEGE OF MUSIC, FIRST DREW THE AUTHOR'S ATTENTION TO THE VITAL IMPORTANCE OF A TRAINED EAR AS THE FOUNDATION OF ALL TRUE MUSICAL EDUCATION, THIS LITTLE WORK, WHICH ADVOCATES THE PLACING OF THE SUBJECT OF EAR-TRAINING IN ITS RIGHT AND LAWFUL POSITION, IS DEDICATED WITH EVERY FEELING OF AFFECTION AND ESTEEM; AND WHILE HE HAS THUS KINDLY PERMITTED HIS NAME TO APPEAR ON THE FIRST PAGE, HIS BRILLIANT GIFTS AS A MUSICIAN HAVE CAUSED IT ALSO TO APPEAR ON THE LAST.

Printed in England

PREFACE.

THE publication of a work upon a subject so interesting and so important as Memory, in its connection with Music and Musical Performance, and about which, as far as the author has been able to discover, absolutely no literature exists, seems to call for no apology. But, because it is the first attempt to deal with this subject, because the territory which the author has endeavoured to map out was largely an unexplored one, in the survey of which he has been obliged to make his own high roads, and erect his own sign posts, he therefore wishes to claim the indulgence of his reader, if, in the investigation which he now presumes to offer to those interested in musical education, his foot has slipped, and he has taken, not perhaps one, but many wrong turnings.

The purpose of this work is chiefly twofold. *First*, it is an inquiry into the various forms of memory employed in piano playing, and the presentation of a theory with regard to the relative extent of the employment of the various forms by different individuals, and whatever be the amount of light or darkness this inquiry may shed upon the subject, the author feels that no earnest and intelligent teacher of the piano can feel altogether uninterested in an attempt, however imperfect and incomplete, to grapple with the unsolved problems which thrust themselves before him at every lesson.

Second, its purpose is to repeat once again, and if possible with stronger emphasis, that oft-told tale that Ear-training, which is largely a cultivation of the musical memory, is THE FACT of all true musical education. Until this is fully recognised and educational and examination schemes modified accordingly, so long will the musical present and future of this country be overshadowed by a dark cloud, which may not affect the flavour of its choicest fruits, but will surely diminish the wealth and richness of its foliage if it does not also mar the beauty and sweetness of its blossoms.

PREFACE.

The book is divided into two parts, each of which is complete in itself, and although it was necessary in the First Part to take some account of the Psychological aspect of the subject, yet the author has endeavoured, as far as possible, to make every Chapter of practical utility and value to the musical student of moderate advancement. For the opinions and theories expressed in this work he accepts the entire responsibility, but at the same time wishes to acknowledge the assistance he has derived from a study of the following works :—" The Senses and the Intellect," Alexander Bain ; " Teacher's Handbook of Psychology," James Sully ; " Elements of Psychology," James Sully ; "Technique and Expression," Franklin Taylor ; " The Art of Music," C. H. Hubert Parry ; and also the valuable suggestions and varied experiences which have been generously placed at his disposal by his friends, Miss Elizabeth Fédarb (who has also supplied the paragraph on the memorizing of Concertos), Dr. Percy Alderson and Mr. John Pointer. The last chapter entitled, " The Memories of Musicians," will be seen to be a collection of the experiences of others, and those who have willingly come forward with help include the names of Sir George Grove, C.B., Miss Constance Bache, Mr. C. Ainslie Barry, Mr. John Bumpus, Mr. F. G. Edwards, the Rev. J. Hampton, and Mr. T. L. Southgate. To all these he owes a debt of gratitude, but especially to Sir George Grove and Mr. C. A. Barry, who have unreservedly placed themselves and their unique knowledge and experiences at his service, not only in connection with the final chapter but throughout the entire work. While to all acknowledging his indebtedness he does not in the least think that by so doing it is in any degree repaid.

The author will be glad to receive communications on the subject, as well as particulars of exceptional performances, which on some future occasion it might be possible to add to the last chapter.

SYDENHAM, *November, 1898.*

TABLE OF CONTENTS.

₊ *The numbers refer to the* Paragraphs, *unless the contrary is stated.*

PART I.

MUSICAL MEMORY, ALSO AN INVESTIGATION INTO THE FORMS OF MEMORY EMPLOYED IN PIANO PLAYING, AND A THEORY AS TO THEIR EMPLOYMENT.

CHAPTER.   PAGE.
I.—GENERAL AND SPECIAL MEMORY   1

The Faculty of Memory and its various divisions, 1. Special Forms of Memory, and to what they are due, 2. The Memory for Colours—for Sounds, 3. To what the natural tastes of an individual are due, 4.

II.—MUSICAL MEMORY   3

Musical Memory defined—its differences in individuals, 5. Its transitory employment by the listener, 6, 7. Its employment for permanent acquisition by the musician, 8-10. Upon what its value depends, 11. Ear-training, 12. Sense of absolute pitch, 13.

III.—MUSICAL MEMORY IN CONNECTION WITH PRACTICAL EXECUTION   ...   8

The memorizing of piano music and the different forms of memory which may be employed, 14-17.

IV.—MUSCULAR MEMORY   10

The Muscular Sense and its retentive power, 18. Reflex Movements, 19. Muscular Memory and Technique, 20, 21. Its employment in memorizing piano music, 22. The form of suitable passages considered, 23-31. Unsuitable passages, 32. The limits of its employment, 33. Its employment in automatic form, 34.

V.—VISUAL MEMORY   19

The different methods of employment, 35. In connection with the *printed page*, 36. In connection with the *keyboard*, 37. The form of suitable and unsuitable passages, 38. The connection between Visual and Muscular Memory, 39. The retention of chords, 40. Visual Control and Visual Memory, 42, 43.

VI.—INTELLECTUAL MEMORY   24

The Intellectual aspect of Music, and how our memory may be employed in connection with it, 44-46. Musical Form, 47-50. The Harmonic basis of passages, 51-53. Elaboration and the forms it assumes, 54-56.

VII.—ON THE RELATIVE EXTENT OF THE EMPLOYMENT OF THE DIFFERENT FORMS OF MEMORY   33

The manner in which the various forms of memory are employed, 58, 59. What influences the employment of the different forms, 60. I. The Nature of the Music to be memorized, 61, 62. II. The Method of Study employed, 63, 64. III. The Peculiarities of the Individual memorizing, 65-67. Suggestions as to a final solution of the problem, 68, 69.

TABLE OF CONTENTS.

PART II.

THE CULTIVATION OF MUSICAL MEMORY.

Chapter.	Page.

VIII.—The Necessity for the Cultivation of Musical Memory ... 38

A trained memory for sounds, a necessary part of every musician's equipment, 70. Ear-training, 71. The power of *reading* music, 72, 73. The *correct* method of studying Harmony, 74. The performance of piano music from memory, 75. Memory playing, a form of mental training, 76. Its injudicious employment, 77.

IX.—General Conditions favourable to Memorizing 41

Mental freshness the first condition, 80–82. Retentive power possessed by the Individual, 83. Power of Concentration, 84–87. Repetition of the Impression, 88.

X.—Some Suggestions for a Scheme of Memory Training 44

State of advancement necessary, 91. The value of early training, 92. Principles which should guide us in the selection of pieces, 93–95 ; as to *Length*, 96—*Form and Construction*, 97, 98—*Detail*, 99—*Difficulty*, 100.

XI.—A Method of Studying Pieces for Memorization 48

How to study a piece *intelligently*, 102, 103. Analysis of the first movement of Beethoven's Sonata in F minor, Op. 2, No. 1, 104-107. The Memorizing of Concertos, 108. Rehearsing from Memory, 109. Mental Rehearsal, 110.

XII.—Memory Training and Examination Schemes 60

The Influence of Examinations, 111-113. The necessity of including Ear-tests in all Harmony Examinations, 114-117. Memory performance in Examinations, 118.

XIII.—The Memories of Musicians 63

A collection of evidences, bearing witness to the possession of remarkable powers of memory by famous musicians, and giving particulars of exceptional memory performances by Mozart, 120. Mendelssohn, 121-123. Ferdinand Hiller, 124. Hans von Bülow, 125, 126, 129. Sir Charles Hallé, with quotations from contemporaneous criticism, 127, 128. Rubenstein, 130. Dr. Hans Richter, 131. Sir Frederick Ouseley, 132, 133. Sir Walter Parratt, 134.

Index to Musical Examples 71

General Index 72

MUSICAL MEMORY.

PART I.

CHAPTER I.

INTRODUCTORY.—GENERAL AND SPECIAL MEMORY.

1. GENERAL AND SPECIAL MEMORY.—The faculty of memory is one of our great primary intellectual powers, and every conscious act, and the large majority of unconscious ones, are the result of the past or present exercise of it. If it were possible for a child to be born absolutely without a memory, it could only become a helpless imbecile, and its life would be a total blank, a darkness to which the darkness of the simply blind would be as brilliant sunshine. Every sane person possesses the power of retention or memory, although individuals exhibit strongly marked differences in the degree to which they possess it. Beyond, however, the difference in the degree of general retentiveness which individuals display, an aptitude for retaining some particular class of impression is often a noticeable feature. Thus, one will be most susceptible to sensations of colour, another to those of form, another to those of sound, and so on; and even with sensations belonging to one class, such as auditory ones, we find that a special power of retention of musical tones does not necessarily carry with it an equal power of retention of articulate sounds as is required in learning to speak a foreign language. From this we see that the faculty of memory is not a simple power, but one which is divisible into as many compartments as there are kinds of impression. These compartments are all more or less independent, and may, and often do, exhibit wide differences both in their original retentive capacity and their subsequent development.

2. SPECIAL MEMORY.—The first step towards the retention of sense-impressions is the accurate perception of them. This depends on the fineness or sensibility of the organ employed; and as a general rule we find that the retentive power of an individual for any special class of impression varies *directly* with the discriminative power of the organ which responds to the particular form of excitement created by the corresponding class of sensation.

3. Let us consider this question for a moment with reference to two of our most valuable organs of sense. The possessor of an eye peculiarly

sensitive to colour, has the different varieties of colour brought vividly before his mind. He is *compelled* to take an interest in all presentations of colour, to notice and take pleasure in the delicate blending of colours, and the harmony which a happy combination of them in room-decoration or personal dress produces; and to feel irritation, and even annoyance at the discord produced by the placing of unsuitable colours in juxtaposition. Thus the interest of such an individual is most easily aroused and sustained when colour-sensations are presented to him, and that which interests one most is most readily and permanently retained. The same is true with reference to the ear. The possessor of an ear specially sensitive to musical sounds has such brought before him in a much stronger and more forcible manner than other sensations. His attention is aroused whenever he hears musical sounds, his interest in them is kindled, instinctively he acquires a liking for and an enjoyment in musical performances, fragments of favourite melodies haunt his mind, and he will be able to concentrate his attention more readily upon sensations of this class, and will therefore retain them with less difficulty and more certainty than any others.

4. In this manner special tastes and special memories are created, and these as a general rule follow local endowments which, if properly developed, may eventually influence the choice of a career or a profession. At the same time the non-possession, in a fairly high degree, of particular powers and their corresponding memories would, in callings in which the exercise of them is vital, prevent the attainment of any high degree of excellence. Perseverance can do many things, but it cannot completely overcome disabilities due to imperfect or non-sensitive natural organs. Both the possession and non-possession of natural gifts should be carefully considered before a profession is finally decided upon.

CHAPTER II.

MUSICAL MEMORY.

5. Musical memory is that particular power by which we retain and can recall at pleasure, a series of musical sounds when presented to us either singly as in a melody, or in combination as in a progression of harmonies. As was stated in the previous chapter, the degree to which this power is possessed by any individual, depends upon the sensibility of the ear, *First*, with regard to the susceptibility of the ear to general sound-sensations, the excitement so caused producing a concentration of mental and nervous force; and *Secondly*, with regard to its special power of discriminating the differences of musical pitch, so that it may readily perceive the difference between various melodies or various harmonies that are presented to it. Considering the marked differences which individuals display in their power of general retentiveness, it is not surprising to find such differences more marked when we come to consider their special memories, and the memory for musical sounds exhibited by different individuals forms no exception to this rule.

6. EMPLOYMENT OF MUSICAL MEMORY BY THE LISTENER.—The extent to which the large majority of people employ this power, and the vital part it plays in making the enjoyment of music possible, is perhaps not always fully appreciated. Unlike Painting and Architecture, which reveal their beauties instantaneously if one has sufficient visual power to perceive them, Music unfolds itself over a space of time, and in its simplest form—a short melody—the various notes are understood only in relation to what has gone before and to what follows. Thus, a fundamental condition of our enjoying music in any degree is the possession of the power of retaining musical sounds, though not necessarily in a high order. The necessity for the exercise of this power is, however, more obvious if we consider the structure or design of a piece of music. The design of a building is exposed to our view in a state of completeness, and if we possess an eye for proportion, a general idea of satisfaction, or the reverse, may be gained instantaneously. With music the case is quite different. The design or form of a piece of music is only intelligible to us if we can retain in our mind some idea of the various portions as they are presented to us, and can compare them with regard to tonality, rhythm, material, and relative importance with what has preceded, and later, with what follows. This is equally true of the simplest satisfactory form one can conceive, such as :—

1st Theme | Contrasted Theme | 1st Theme repeated. ||

as of the most elaborate movement by Beethoven. All music demands alike for its intelligent hearing an exercise of musical memory, although in immensely different degrees.

7. A study of the Sonata-form movements of Beethoven, and a comparison of the "first portion" with the "recapitulation" will show us how in the latter (which in earlier composers was mere repetition), the composer delighted to introduce surprises of every description, which, however, can only be fully appreciated and understood by the retentive listener. The following bars from the "Waldstein" Sonata will instantly occur to the mind of many pianists, where the last note in Ex. Ia at first almost appears to have the character of a wrong note until the insistence of the passage in this form in the following bars, banishes such an impression and reveals the substitution of A flat for G at such a striking point as being one of the composer's bold and daring methods of arresting the attention, and sustaining the interest of the listener. But for one who has retained no idea of the first version of the passage (Ex. I) the second version can have no such revelation, and therefore far less meaning.

Another exceptionally fine instance, where Beethoven seems to have set himself to shock his pedantic listeners, quite as much as to mystify the unpedantic ones, may be seen in the Sonata in D minor, Op. 31, No. 2, if the opening of the first movement is compared with the beginning of the recapitulation. Not merely, however, in listening to movements in which there is repetition of previous material do we have to exercise our memory, but works which are evolved from one theme—such as Fugues, sets of Variations, and some modern Rhapsodies—lose all their significance and meaning, unless we can frequently compare the present with the past; while in Opera and Oratorio, the *leit motiv* is a device which appeals to the same power. The intelligent listener must be constantly employing his memory even when hearing works of simple and obvious construction, while for the understanding of compositions of greater calibre and deeper meaning, a severe effort of memory is often absolutely necessary.

8. MUSICAL MEMORY EMPLOYED FOR PERMANENT ACQUISITION.—From a consideration of the transitory memory necessary to the listener we will now pass and proceed to trace briefly the development of musical memory for the purpose of permanent acquisition. The early growth of musical memory becomes manifest when a child, whose interest has been aroused by the hearing of some pretty tune, will

recognise it upon a subsequent appearance and even attempt to sing or hum it to himself. A child with a sensitive ear may give frequent exhibitions of this kind, reproducing in a fragmentary manner, although often with considerable accuracy, tunes he has heard in school, in church, or in the drawing-room. Often he has quite a store of melodic treasures long before he is taught to sing a major scale, the material of which he has been unconsciously employing for some time previously. A child's introduction to, and memorization of the Major scale, supplies him with the tonal foundation or basis of the greater part of music. If the ear is of average sensibility, and has been previously exercised in gathering fragments of tunes, this acquisition of the complete major scale presents little or no difficulty. On the other hand, the possessor of an ear which is less sensitive, and which has had little past experience, must carefully study and memorize the intervals between the adjacent notes, as well as the order of their progression, before he can recall it at any time with absolute accuracy.

9. Following upon the acquisition of the intervals of the major scale in gradual progression, the next step is the memorization of the intervals formed by its several notes not adjacent to one another. To have done this successfully really means that we have still more indelibly memorized the several notes of the scale, so that we can bring it instantly before our minds, not only as a whole, but as to any of its individual members which may be distantly situated from one another, without the aid of the intervening notes. In other words, we have familiarized ourselves with all the different intervals of the major scale. The memorization of the Minor scale with its characteristic intervals is a subsequent, as well as a more difficult operation, whilst the accurate memorization of the Chromatic scale is a task of great difficulty even to trained musicians.

10. The power to memorize notes in combination or chords, is a proof of the possession of a fairly high grade of musical intelligence. Such ability must be possessed in some degree by every one laying claim to the title of musician. As the harmony student has the different varieties of chords brought before him, if he does not already know them by sound, he must memorize the sound of each chord, at the same time as he studies its intervals, and *before* he studies its special treatment in any detail.

11. UPON WHAT THE VALUE OF MUSICAL MEMORY DEPENDS.—The value of any form of memory depends entirely upon our ability not only to recall, but to reproduce and to employ in some form or other what we have stored on previous occasions. In the very large majority of facts about our life and experience, the powers of speech and written language are the media by which we convey our knowledge to others, and as a great portion of our early education is devoted to gaining proficiency in these, the possibility of dissociating the power of memory from the power of reproducing what is retained, may never occur to us, much less the possibility of our being unable to convey to others what we can remember, simply because we are unacquainted with any method or language by means of which we can interpret it to

them. This, however, is no impossible situation to be in with regard to impressions of musical sounds which we may have stored. Many people who can remember with a fair amount of accuracy the melody or a portion of the melody of a simple song, are quite unable to write down with any degree of correctness what they remember, either because they do not understand the signs of musical notation, or if they do understand them, are unable to associate them with what they hear or with what they have retained from hearing in the past. In other words, they are unable to associate the *sounds* with the corresponding *signs*.

12. It will be seen, therefore, that the value of musical memory depends very largely upon our ability to classify what we retain upon some intelligible and generally recognised plan, and to record it in a language both definite and well understood; and this will imply the possession of the complementary power of reading (that is, hearing in our minds) music written in this same language. How this object may be obtained, seems to us to consist in the adoption in musical education of a complete and comprehensive system of ear-training, educating the ear to discriminate different rhythms, intervals, and chords, the memory to retain the sound of such, and the intellect to classify them and associate such classification with the signs of some form of musical notation. Scales, intervals and chords represent the raw material of music, and he who can retain all the varieties of such possesses the material of musical composition. Whether he can fashion them into intelligible musical thought depends upon his knowledge of what may be called the Technique of Composition in its widest sense.

Many persons who are quite ignorant of musical notation, and who have never attempted to seriously study music, are able by means of a quick and retentive ear and a certain facility of finger to reproduce upon some musical instrument (generally the piano), passages which have attracted their attention. Such efforts are commonly described as "playing by ear." Without attempting to despise such a power, for it reveals the possession of natural gifts of a fairly high order, we cannot but regret that the lack of any serious purpose which such performances frequently display, bears witness to the absence of other powers which are necessary, before natural abilities may become of true and lasting value.

13. SENSE OF ABSOLUTE PITCH.—In our consideration of the memorization of intervals and chords, we have always meant it to be inferred that the pitch of the notes of such was relative to some given or assumed sound and not in any sense absolute. The majority of people do not possess what is called a "sense of absolute pitch," but the fact of its existence demands that we should not pass unnoticed what is really an exceptionally perfect form of musical memory. It is apparently due to the possession of an ear of a peculiarly sensitive and retentive nature, which has the power of seizing upon definite sounds, and by the remarkably acute susceptibility of the mind to sound-sensation has ingrained them so effectually, that they have become permanent or fixed ideas of pitch. With some who possess this power it is partly the result of special sensibility, and partly the result of the constant repetition of one particular sound which has eventually become permanent, and forms a basis from which they calculate, perhaps

almost unconsciously, other sounds. This is sometimes the case with choristers, who, by singing at daily church or cathedral services, acquire a fixed impression of their intoning note, while players of string instruments often permanently memorize their "A" for a similar reason, but such acquired pitches are apt to disappear or become uncertain when frequency of repetition is interrupted or altogether ceases. The fact that many highly trained musicians do not possess this sense of absolute pitch, while many persons, otherwise unmusical do, proves it to be a natural and accidental fineness of ear with a peculiar retentive capacity for definite pitch, which does not necessarily carry with it anything else characteristic of the musician. Like other powers it generally appears first as a germ, which must be judiciously exercised and developed in order to be brought to maturity, and its growth may be rapid or slow according to the endowments of the individual. The remarkably early age at which it sometimes manifests itself in a high degree of perfection, of which Mozart was a notable example, bears evidence to the possession of phenomenal gifts rather than to any exception in the law of development of the intellectual powers.

CHAPTER III.

MUSICAL MEMORY IN CONNECTION WITH PRACTICAL EXECUTION.

14. Hitherto we have considered the faculty of Musical Memory in what may be termed its purely mental manifestations, and quite apart from its employment in connection with practical execution. We shall now consider it in relation to that; and we have chosen the piano as our single representative instrument on account of its popularity, although many of the principles stated with special reference to piano-playing may be readily adapted to the requirements of the modes of execution belonging to other musical instruments.

15. The question which now presents itself for solution is this:— Assuming a pianist to possess the necessary powers for playing a piece from memory, does he, as far as the memorization of it is concerned, rely entirely upon the power of pure musical memory which we have described in the previous chapter? Does he retain each and every individual sound in his mind and translate them on to the keyboard as he progresses? Before we can attempt to answer this question we must glance at the operation of pianoforte playing. The playing of the piano is a most complex act. It is possible for our fingers, ears, eyes and intellect to be all more or less actively engaged throughout the progress of a piece. Now, as a result of this, when we desire to play from memory, the forms of memory belonging to these various powers are all available in some degree for the purpose. Such being the case, it would be unusual to find one special form altogether relied upon, but rather two or three operating simultaneously, assisting and controlling one another, although perhaps, to us, almost unconsciously. It is possible for pianists who possess an ear of ideal sensibility and retentive power, to retain elaborate and lengthy compositions, with all their details, entirely by their unaided musical memory; and, provided their powers of execution and concentration are of an equally high order, their performances would probably be an instantaneous translation of the mental picture they possess on to the keyboard. But as of the many pianists who play from memory, a small minority possess an ear which, both by natural fineness and subsequent training, is equal to such a task, it is evident that many cannot rely absolutely on any single form of musical memory.

16. Considering, however, the possibility of the employment of several widely contrasted forms of memory, it is not surprising to find that those who play from memory frequently possess no exact knowledge of the

forms they do employ, or the extent to which they employ them. In some passages they think they rely more upon one form than another, as in the playing of a brilliant arpeggio, which the fingers having traversed many times, eventually come to play quite automatically, though it would be exceptional not to find that same passage memorized also by some other form of memory, so that if our so-called "finger" memory should temporarily fail, the other form could come to its assistance. But whatever be the amount of assistance supplied by these non-musical forms of memory, it is obvious that our musical memory must still supply us with a clear general idea of the piece we are playing, and our ear must exercise throughout its course a criticism of its rhythm, the accuracy of its notes, gradations of tone and interpretation.

17. In the following chapters we shall consider separately the forms of memory belonging to the Muscular Sense (by which we control the movements of the fingers, the hand and the arm for the purpose of execution), the Eye, and the Intellect, in their connection with the performance from memory of piano music, as well as the special province and the particular kind of passage most suited to each form of memory, and shall then endeavour to ascertain if there be any principle or law to which the employment of the various forms in different individuals conform.

CHAPTER IV.

MUSCULAR MEMORY.

18. As by the aid of Verbal memory we can retain successions of words, and by Musical memory successions of notes and harmonies, so by the power of memory possessed by our Muscular sense, we are able to retain trains or successions of movements. It is a law of our Intellect that movements, like other forms of sensation, occurring in close succession, tend to bind themselves together; so that after a series has been repeated many times, the revival of one movement will probably revive, in correct order, any others which may follow. We know that the opening phrase of a melody will bring the whole strain before the mind, and that a line of poetry will often recall a stanza; and this "Law of Contiguity," as it is called by Psychologists, is not less true in connection with our Muscular sense or when applied to a series of movements.

19. REFLEX MOVEMENTS.—But with movements we can proceed further than simply memorising them, so that they can be reproduced by a continuous effort of Will for that special purpose. We can by sufficient repetition gradually convert them into automatic, mechanical or, correctly speaking, reflex actions; that is, we can employ them and rely upon the accurate performance of them while other matters are engrossing our attention. An immense number of our actions, which at one time demanded special care and attention before they could be accurately performed, have by repetition been converted into unconscious or reflex ones. An example is supplied by the movements employed in dancing. Such a complicated step as that of the Waltz, which is acquired only after much careful repetition, is eventually employed with the greatest accuracy and certainty, quite unconsciously and mechanically, and while the attention is devoted entirely to other matters. When for the performance of a series of movements, voluntary attention becomes absolutely unnecessary, such movements may be said to be perfectly acquired.

20. MUSCULAR MEMORY AND TECHNIQUE.—In learning to play upon a musical instrument like the piano, which requires rapid and accurate finger movements, the acquisition and memorization of such enters very largely into what is known as the Technical side of our studies. Our earliest efforts are directed to secure correct finger-movements for striking the keys when the hand is in an easy and natural position (five-finger exercises). From this we proceed to acquire facility in making similar movements when the hand is either extended, contracted, or in the position for passing the thumb under (broken chords, scales, etc.), and our frequent repetition of these exercises, and similar ones of a more advanced nature, is not only to enable us to gain perfect control over the

muscles which control our hand and fingers, but also, as a result of the frequent repetition of the same series of movements, to enable our muscular sense eventually to memorize those series of movements which are most frequently employed in piano playing, the perfect and instinctive performance of which is the foundation of all good technique. These trains and successions of movements are, as it were, stored up, in order that they may be ready for use when required, and employed with the least possible effort, or even without conscious effort, and they represent the foundation upon which still more difficult and complicated movements are built. In studying, therefore, the technique of new pieces, the difficulties we have to overcome are the adaptation of previously acquired successions of movements to new figures, and the acquisition of new series.

21. From this it will be seen how very largely the cultivation and exercise of the muscular memory enters into the study of piano playing, and it is only to those who possess a delicate muscular sense, that any high degree of proficiency therein is possible. The power of producing beautiful tone and its many varieties which characterize expressive and finished playing depends, after the possession of a fine ear, entirely upon the possession of a delicate muscular sense, which has been trained until it is under complete control. By the natural possession of such, many are able to acquire in a few months a control in tone-production which others are unable to acquire in a lifetime; and in the muscular sense as in other senses, where a special delicacy of discrimination of movement exists, a special retentiveness for such will be found to co-exist.

22. It is impossible to say how far piano music can be memorized simply by the aid of muscular memory, as the movements must always be associated with some other forms of sensation, such as touch, sound, and generally sight, all of which greatly assist in linking the movements together; but few will deny that in performing music from memory, especially that of a rapid and brilliant nature, the assistance which can be supplied by this form of memory is invaluable and almost unlimited in extent. In our present consideration of muscular memory, we shall, however, always regard it as a supplementary form with which other forms of memory are working simultaneously, and which exercise over it a certain amount of control and guidance; and we shall limit our attention to a consideration of those forms of passage which we consider specially secure when memorized by the sense under discussion, without in any way denying the possibility of memorizing other passages by this same power.

23. PASSAGES SUITABLE TO BE MEMORIZED BY MUSCULAR MEMORY. —It must be obvious that the general style of passages most readily and securely memorized by means of muscular memory, or as it is often yet less correctly called " Finger-memory," will be such as require rapid and precise finger movements, and especially what may be termed "brilliant" passages, that is, extended passages founded on scales and arpeggios, and requiring for their performance a strong, clear touch. It is not infrequently the case, that after learning to play a piece composed of difficult passages of this class, with which are

interspersed less difficult passages of a perhaps more *cantabile* nature, we find we can play the difficult portions from memory but not the other portions. This is due to the greater number of repetitions which the former have required and received, with the result, that, without any special wish or desire on our part, our muscular sense has memorized the entire series of movements, and as soon as the start is given, the fingers and hand are unerringly guided over the whole passage with the least amount of voluntary or conscious control, or perhaps without any. *When such passages progress in a systematic form, and are constructed upon some pattern extending over an octave, so as to admit of a regular method of fingering, employing the majority of the fingers, and affording little opportunity for them either to operate in the wrong order or to make a false movement, such passages belong to the class most securely memorized by muscular memory.* For the sake of convenience we shall describe these as belonging to *Class I*.

24. CLASS I.—This class will include most scale passages of considerable extent belonging to *one* form of the normal scale. Such fulfil all the requisite conditions, in addition to having had the necessary movements acquired in our technical studies. The points which require our attention are the scale to which the passage belongs and the initial and final notes :—

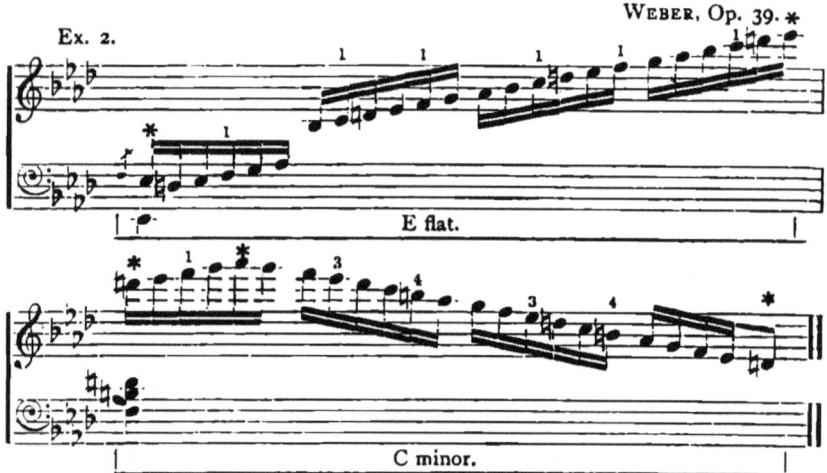

When a scale passage leaves one form of scale by introducing notes foreign to that form, and becomes a mixture of two forms, as major and chromatic :—

or minor and chromatic, the points where it differs from the form which chiefly prevails must be carefully noted and retained by some other form of memory. Should the order of the progression established in one octave be repeated in subsequent octaves :—

the task is considerably lighter than when no such regularity prevails. But in every instance we should associate it primarily with that normal form which it most closely resembles, in order that we may have the smallest number of differences to remember *intellectually.**

25. This method of memorizing scale passages is only suitable in its application to passages of considerable extent, and that move in one direction for some length of time. Scale passages in which the direction of the movement changes every few notes, as in Ex. 5 :—

will generally be found to be based upon some progression of chords, and the bass of this progression will often supply a rough outline of the moving part. In such passages the memorization of the harmonic framework is the safest method of procedure.

* The principle of reducing everything to its smallest and simplest form will be more fully discussed in Chapter VI, on Intellectual Memory.

26. In addition to scale passages, to Class I also belong passages in "grand arpeggio" form, where the same figure, and consequently the same finger-movements are repeated through several octaves.

27. Passages of hardly less security than these, and which may be included in the same class, are those constructed upon a figure recurring at smaller intervals than that of an octave, but which employ almost identical series of finger movements. Ex 7 is a type of such, and the Finale of Beethoven's Sonata in A flat, Op. 26, contains many similar passages. To remember their harmonic framework is a precautionary measure :—

28. Already we have had to refer to the harmonic basis of passages as something from which the student may derive valuable assistance, and it may be well to state once for all, that we shall assume our reader possesses a reasonable acquaintance with the subject of Harmony, the value of which to every musical student needs no advocacy from us.

29. We now come to the next class of passage which can be memorized largely by means of muscular memory.

CLASS II, *comprises passages evolved from a figure or pattern, which figure, however, both in its form and progression, accomodates itself to the harmonic structure of the passage.*

The greater the irregularity of a passage, the larger number of repetitions does it require before the series of movements are securely memorized ; if, however, we can discover some principle of construction running throughout the passage, and to which we can reduce its apparent irregularities, we shall have found out that which will not merely help us in reading the passage, but also which will greatly add to our security when memorizing it.

The following will illustrate this form of passage:—

When memorizing these and all similar passages, we should first reduce them to their simplest harmonic basis (Exs. 8a and 9a), and then note the principle upon which the figure of the passage is formed, that is, the order in which the essential and auxiliary notes occur. (See Chap. VI)

Class II will also include passages like the following:—

where the figure is modified to suit, not the different intervals of the same chord but those of another chord, the passage being founded on a progression of chords. A memorization of this progression (Ex. 10 a), is a great assistance towards a memorization of the elaborated form.

30. The above passage (Ex. 10) continued to the 14th bar from that which we have numbered 1, affords an excellent example of passages in which, with regard to some points, the reliance upon muscular memory is unsafe. Confining our attention to the treble part, we see that bars 1 to 7 are repeated an octave lower in bars 8 to 14, with the exception of the first figure of 6 notes in bars 3 and 5, corresponding to the first figure in bars 10 and 12.

Ex. 11.

The alteration in the form of the figure is the same in both cases, and this somewhat simplifies matters; *but in the memorization of this passage, and all others which start alike but differ in the course of their progress, we must retain all such differences mentally, and rigorously control our muscular memory at every place where there is a likelihood of a false step.*

31. CLASS III.—*The last class which we have to consider in connection with this form of memory comprises passages which are not constructed upon any regular figure, or if some design does underlie them, the imitations of it are of such an uncertain character that they may be legitimately described as irregular.*

Many passages belonging to this class demand for their performance considerable extension of the hand and fingers, and also in their progress traverse a large portion of the keyboard,

CHOPIN, Op. 52.

Ex. 12.

and, as a consequence of their difficulty, receive in practice a far greater number of repetitions than passages of simpler and more obvious construction. Thus we often memorize such passages by muscular memory in merely learning to play them with ease and accuracy, and even when the music is before us, we frequently play such from memory;

that is, we look at the keyboard and not at the music, in order that we may exercise an amount of *visual control* over the performance of them. (Chap. V).

32. In passages of the style described above, the chance of confusion arising with regard to the finger movements is slight, such, however, is not the case with irregular figures and passages which circle chiefly around a comparatively few and closely situated notes, keeping the hand in a contracted rather than in an extended condition. The employment of a large number of simple and similar movements occurring closely upon one another as in Chopin's Etude, Op. 25, No. 2 :—

Ex. 13.

admits of a greater possibility of confusion in reproducing them chiefly by the aid of muscular memory than when the series of movements are more strongly defined, and more widely separated. A condition which adds to the security of muscular memory in passages like the above-mentioned, is the ability to employ as many different fingers as possible, provided, of course, that the employment of them is in accordance with a good system of fingering. A series of movements starting, say, with the first finger, is less likely to become confused with the next series starting from the same finger if, between the two appearances of this finger, there are three of the other fingers employed instead of only one or two.

33. The three classes into which we have broadly divided brilliant piano passages, have merely brought into prominence particular forms of passage for which our muscular memory may be relied upon with a large amount of security. Theoretically speaking, any passage of unbroken finger movements of moderate extent can be memorized by this form of memory; but this is far from saying that all such are suitable. Series of slow finger movements cohere together with less certainty than series of quick movements. Besides this, in slow *cantabile* passages, we do not require so much the assistance of muscular-memory, as such passages are more readily retained by some other power. Notwithstanding this, the suggestions of muscular-memory are often valuable even in passages of slow *tempo*, although in such cases the assistance rendered is of a far less vital character than in passages in quick *tempo*.

34. Before quitting this subject we may draw attention to the fact, that in playing passages in which the part for one hand has say, three

notes, against two or four in the part for the other hand, we may employ in one hand muscular-memory in an almost automatic form, whilst we devote the greater part of our attention to the performance of the other. Thus the bass of Chopin's Fantasie-Impromptu, the treble of the development of the first movement of Beethoven's Sonata in G, Op. 14, No. 2, beginning :—

and many like passages would possibly be played in this manner

CHAPTER V.

VISUAL MEMORY.

35. The power of memory possessed by the eye may be employed to assist the pianist in two quite different ways. It may retain the image of the printed book, or it may retain the image of the notes upon the keyboard. On the other hand its assistance can be wholly dispensed with, as is proved by the number of blind pianists, some of no mean ability.

36. RETENTION OF A MENTAL PICTURE OF THE PRINTED PAGE.—How far it is possible to retain by this form of memory an accurate mental picture of a page, or of many different pages of printed music, with all their elaborate and complicated details, will depend upon the special memory for *Forms* which an individual may possess, but we cannot conceive the task of memorizing by this method the music of modern composers, with all its wealth of detail, to be otherwise than a laborious one, and one which the pianist of average ability will be likely to employ to any very great extent. It is true we can often recall the general outline of a piece, and perhaps some of its more prominent details, by associating them with their position on the different pages; but the pianist with an ordinary memory for printed symbols will probably not remember much more than this by this form of memory. When a piece is thoroughly memorized, it is by no means impossible or even particularly difficult to revive it mentally in its printed form, but this may be done largely by the aid of other forms of memory, and our Visual memory may render little vital assistance. As a general rule those who possess this particular form of memory in a high degree, will soon discover the fact and make use of their possession. Those who do not will find that for musical purposes the cultivation of other forms is more remunerative.

37. RETENTION OF A MENTAL PICTURE OF THE PROGRESSION ON THE KEYBOARD.—In addition to its power of retaining the symbols of musical notation, the Visual memory can also retain the order of the progression of the notes on the keyboard. In the earliest stages of pianoforte playing, the beginner learns to name the different notes correctly by recognising their position in relation to the grouping of the black notes. When this stage is passed he has to associate them with their position on the stave, and to play exercises of simple progressions from printed music. Here, two difficulties confront him, first—that of translating the musical notation on to the keyboard, and second—that of making correct finger movements. Until he has had considerable practice, he cannot, without looking, judge the requisite

stretch of the hand, nor the position of the finger required in order to strike accurately notes separated by an interval of several notes. But, as the habit of looking at the keyboard, if too freely indulged in, is a bar to progress in sight reading, the teacher must be careful not to allow the keyboard to monopolize more attention than is absolutely necessary to secure accurate movements, and to gradually reduce the attention in this direction, as the hand and fingers become more secure in their movements, and more completely under voluntary control. The tendency of beginners to play their pieces largely by the aid of visual memory, that is, by remembering the order of the notes on the keyboard, is the greatest possible hindrance in sight-reading, but when considerable advancement in execution and sight-reading has been made, this question of visual memory, loses its importance as hindering progress, and we may find this form one which we shall employ but to a very limited extent.

38. A method for accurately estimating the amount of assistance which this, or any other form of memory may contribute to the complex act of memorizing, is as far as possible to consider such in isolation, and apart from its combination and co-operation with other forms of memory. For this purpose let us take a dumb keyboard, and try to memorize some passage of single notes and of moderate length, not by means of the printed music, but by seeing some other person play it upon this keyboard. In this case, assuming that a knowledge of Harmony does not exist, we have a task which exercises merely our power of remembering the order of the notes upon the keyboard by the aid of visual memory. We are appealing to the eye, and therefore the regular distribution of colour (black and white), and the repetition of a figure or pattern, will represent the simplest exercises for this form of memory. Thus, scale passages, grand arpeggios and all other passages based upon the recurrence of some established pattern, are easily retained. Ex. 15 illustrates this :—

Ex. 15.   CHOPIN, Op. 31.

modulates back to C, repeating the first melody and then the second one, both in the key of C, in which key it concludes." To one who is accustomed to consider the form of compositions, this description would produce some such mental picture as the following :—

Key C.	Key G.	Key C.	Key C.
1st Subject.	2nd Subject.	1st Subject.	2nd Subject.

which, in the terminology of musical form, might be described as an example of the binary form in miniature. Although we may know absolutely nothing about the materials and details of the piece briefly described above, yet a clear perception of its general outline, which is obtained from a knowledge of the order of the appearances of the themes and the sequence of the keys, is a help both to its intelligent study and memorization. Some may argue that the large majority of pieces proceed in such a manner as to prevent the possibility of confusion between appearances of the same passage in different keys. This is undoubtedly true, but it is also true that no small number of pieces exist, in which, if we have not a clear idea of the sequence of the keys definitely fixed in our mind, in playing from memory, a moment's inattention will make a serious error possible. Thus, what may be called the second subject of the "Aufschwung," from Schumann's "Phantasiestücke," appears first in D flat, and then in the recapitulation in A flat, although the passage and cadence which precedes it is identical on both occasions.

Ex. 20.   Schumann, Op. 12, No. 2.

Ex. 20 a.

A similar instance will be seen on a comparison of bars 16 and 113 of "Grillen" from the same set of pieces, and the following from the Finale of Beethoven's Sonata in C minor, Op. 10, No. 1, is another :—

Such passages may be regarded as the exception rather than the rule, and we admit they do not form the majority, but it is the obviousness of those cited rather than any essential difference which distinguishes them from many other passages like the following from Brahms' Rhapsody in B Minor, the security of which depends upon a recognition of the same principle :—

48. THE "METHODS" OF BEETHOVEN.—Not only, however, in the general design of movements which are built upon some clear and definite plan can we enlist the services of Intellectual memory, but it can be brought to our assistance also in the parts of movements which from their very nature are, to some extent irregular, as in the "development" of Sonata-form movements. Beethoven, beyond all other composers has shown how this portion of a movement, though quite free and unfettered in its progress, may yet be made in the highest sense coherent and satisfactory by the employment of various devices, which are valuable from an emotional point of view as they are intelligent from an intellectual one. To discuss the nature of such in any degree of detail belongs to a treatise on Musical Composition and not to a handbook on Musical Memory, but for the benefit of those who have not yet critically studied Beethoven's "methods," we will draw attention to a few of these devices, not regarding our reader as a student of composition, but as one who when playing from memory is desirous of making his performance secure by the co-operation of as many forms of memory as is possible, and who recognises that the perception of such devices adds to this security.

49. Perhaps the most prominent of such devices is *a regular progression of the bass of the harmonic foundation, either descending or ascending.* The *descent* of the bass in stepwise progression is illustrated at the beginning of the development of the first movement of the Sonata in G major, Op. 31, No. 1, and also in the development of the first movement of the

Sonata in B flat, Op. 22, beginning at the 24th bar after the double bar. A corresponding *ascent* of the bass may be seen in the first movement of the Sonata in D minor, Op. 31, No. 2, beginning at bar 21, and in the transposition of this passage in the development portion, where the bass ascends stepwise, first at distances of four bars and afterwards at distances of two bars. Another and similar example will be found in this same Sonata in the development of the last movement, where at bar 32 after the double bar, the bass ascends from the lower C to the B flat above. This ascent also proceeds first at intervals of four bars, and afterwards at shorter distances. But the finest example of such a device is in the development of the first movement of the Sonata "Appassionata," where the bass ascends from the lower D flat gradually for two octaves, and then by minor 3rds for another two octaves, finally descending by 3rds throughout the whole four octaves.

50. A device of another kind is *regularity in the sequence of keys.* This may be seen in the development of the first movement of the Sonata in E flat, Op. 31, No. 3, where, beginning at the 12th bar after the double bar, it proceeds through keys at the distance of a 4th, that is, in the relationship of Dominant to Tonic. Another example is the development of the first movement of the Sonata in A flat, Op. 110, where a descending melodic sequence in the treble takes place simultaneously with a progression of keys descending in 3rds (F Minor, D flat, B flat Minor). Another instance of the employment of 3rds in regulating the progression of keys, but this time ascending, may be seen in the "second subject" of the first movement of the Sonata in A major, Op. 2, No. 2. Many instances of the employment of other forms of sequence could be quoted from Beethoven's works, it may therefore be more interesting and instructive to give, as a concluding example, one from the works of another composer of quite different methods and genius. In Ex. 23 we see a real sequence of four bars rising a tone at each occurence. The sequence really begins eight bars before what is here printed, but this extract will be sufficient to illustrate our point.

Ex. 23. CHOPIN, Op. 31.

It should now be obvious how a clear intellectual grasp of the form of a piece, and of some of the more prominent devices, methods of construction and important modulations, will greatly assist us when memorizing it.

51. (II) HARMONIC BASIS.—The greater portion of piano music is the presentation, in an elaborated form, of a more or less simple harmonic basis; and our present purpose is to show how to discover this basis, which may be memorized as the foundation upon which to build the required elaborations. The form of the elaborations and the principles upon which they progress will be considered later.

Our method of procedure will be to make two subdivisions: (1) Elaborations evolved from *a single chord*, and (2) Elaborations evolved from *a progression of chords*.

52. ELABORATIONS EVOLVED FROM A SINGLE CHORD.—Perhaps of all recognized piano compositions, those of Mendelssohn exhibit this form of elaboration—that is, brilliant passages created out of simple chords, to the greatest extent. We have therefore chosen an example from the Sonata in G minor by Schumann, a composer whose methods are as a general rule more recondite.

By comparing Ex. 24 with the harmonic framework as printed below (Exs. 24, a and b), we shall see that the whole passage is but an elaboration of the chord of the diminished 7th on F sharp, the fourth note in each group of semiquavers being an auxiliary note resolving on to the first note of the following group, and a clear recognition of all this will both facilitate and add security to the memorization of it. The following example from the "Andantino" of the same Sonata may also be analysed and studied in a similar manner:—

Ex. 25

Ex. 25 a.   Ex. 25 b.

To memorize this framework (Ex. 25 a) no great effort will be required, and when this is done, the memorization of the auxiliary notes required to complete the passage, when the relationship of the auxiliary and essential notes is clearly understood, will present little difficulty.

53. ELABORATIONS EVOLVED FROM A PROGRESSION OF CHORDS.—In many passages belonging to this class, the chords and their progression are indicated by the part for the left hand, but in the following example—as well as in others which might be taken from the same work—such is not the case, and the harmonic basis is therefore less obvious.

Ex. 26.   CHOPIN, Op. 20.

Ex. 26 a.

In this and similar passages, the memorization of the harmonic basis will form a secure foundation upon which other forms of memory may build.

54. (III) FORM AND PROGRESSION OF ELABORATION.—The consideration of this, the last chief division of our subject, compels us at the outset to notice two distinct features. (1) The principle upon which the elaboration is formed, and (2) if such be in the form of a figure, repeated at regular intervals, the principle which governs its progress.

55. PRINCIPLE OF ELABORATION.—Such may be in accordance with one of the recognised forms of broken chords, as in the following extract :—

Ex. 27.   BEETHOVEN, Op. 2, No. 3.

or it may be such as includes the employment of auxiliary notes alternated with essential notes, as in the "cadenza" of this same movement, where the outline in Ex. 28 a is elaborated into Ex. 28, simply by the employment of what are technically called "changing notes," or auxiliary notes, employed both above and below the essential notes :—

Ex. 28.

Ex. 28 a.

Elaboration consists chiefly of the regular and irregular employment of auxiliary notes in connection with essential notes. When such employment occurs at regular intervals, a pattern or figure is the result, as in Ex. 30. The simplest form of such elaboration is when the several notes of a chord are spread in arpeggio, and each preceded by an auxiliary note, as in Ex. 29. The best method of memorizing such a passage seems to be, first, to regard it in its plain form, Ex. 29 a, and then, recognising the principle upon which the elaboration is framed, to add it afterwards (as in Ex. 25). In the following passage every second note will be seen to consist of a lower auxiliary note resolving on an essential note a semitone higher:—

Ex. 29.   WEBER, Op. 39.

Ex. 29 a.

In cases where a figure or pattern is formed, as in Ex. 30, the relative position of the auxiliary note in the figure should be noted.

56. THE PROGRESSION OF FIGURES.—The progression of a figure may be either (*a*) scalewise, (*b*) according to the intervals of a chord, or (*c*) according to some other regularly recurring interval. In either case such progression may be retained intellectually. Ex. 30 shows a figure whose initial notes proceed according to the scale of D minor:—

Ex. 30.   SCHUBERT, Op. 15.

In Ex. 31, as well as in other passages which closely follow it in the Sonata, the progression is according to the notes of a chord—in this case the Dominant 7th on G :—

Ex. 31.   BEETHOVEN, Op. 57.

In Exs. 27 and 28 this same principle of progression is also illustrated.
Our last example shows a figure repeated at the interval of ascending 4ths :—

Ex. 32.   SCHUMANN, Op. 4, No. 2.

57. In this chapter we have drawn attention to a few of the aspects of musical material which appeal to the Intellect, and have brought into prominence some of the methods which may be employed in analysing and studying such for memorization. But as we previously stated, the extent to which the student will be able thus to memorize passages intellectually, will depend entirely upon his knowledge of Harmony, Form, and the Theory of Music generally.

CHAPTER VII.

ON THE RELATIVE EXTENT OF THE EMPLOYMENT OF THE DIFFERENT FORMS OF MEMORY.

58. In the previous chapters we have considered the various forms of memory by which we are able to memorize piano music for performance, as well as the passages most suited to each form, and the reason of such suitability; and the most casual reader must have noticed, that there are very few passages which cannot be memorized by several different forms of memory. It was seen that the various forms do not exercise themselves over separate provinces having clearly defined boundaries, but rather, that there was one common ground over which, with certain limitations, all had a right of way, and which it was possible for all to traverse at the same moment, though perhaps not with equal facility.

59. While admitting this we must, however, never lose sight of the fact that Music appeals primarily to our sense of hearing, and that the pre-eminent characteristic of a musician should be the possession of a trained and sensitive ear and a corresponding memory for musical sounds. In memory-playing, the memory of the ear therefore is the form which one might naturally expect to bear the greatest amount of responsibility. Yet there are many good musicians and other capable executants, who are unable to trust their unaided ear to remember all the details of a long and complicated composition; while we believe that some who play piano music from memory, hardly rely upon their ear at all to *supply* information with respect to the notes. Therefore, although our investigation into the forms of memory employed is completed, we are still confronted with this not unimportant nor uninteresting question,—What influences the selection and employment of the other forms of memory which help us to complete the task that is beyond the unaided power of the ear to accomplish? Is there any Intellectual law which controls such selection, or is it purely the result of circumstances of an accidental and capricious nature?

To a brief discussion of this problem we shall now address ourselves, and endeavour to place before our readers some conclusions which we have come to on this subject and which to us seem neither unreasonable nor unsatisfactory. If they supply but "the feeblest light, or even so much as a more precise recognition of the darkness which is the first step to attainment of light," we believe they will not be unwelcome.

60. In playing piano music from memory the selection and employment of some special forms of memory in preference to other possible forms can only be due to the influence of one or more of the following conditions. *First*, The nature of the music itself. *Second*, The method of study employed. *Third*, The peculiarities of the individual memorizing. These three conditions cover the whole ground, and if we can eliminate from them all the circumstances which are of a varying and

capricious nature, what is left must form the basis upon which any ultimate principle of selection, if such exists, must rest. With this object in view we will proceed to consider each possible source of influence separately.

61. Our First condition referring to the NATURE OF THE MUSIC TO BE MEMORIZED, includes not only a recognition of the peculiar character of Music as organised sounds, but also of such other special features thereof as may be brought into prominence when it is played upon a keyboard instrument like the piano, and may therefore in performance be brought into contact with other forms of memory such as Muscular Memory. Music addresses its universal appeal to the ear, while the moulding of its materials appeals to the intellect of the musically educated. Any ultimate principle of selection must therefore first and foremost be consistent when applied to facts which refer to the very essence and nature of music. Again, when music is considered with reference to performance on the piano, complete control over certain parts of the muscular organism is a vital condition of success. Another fact therefore which our ultimate principle must recognize is the indispensible conditions of musical performance. Both of these are too obviously fundamental to need further discussion.

62. Besides these two sources of influence, our first condition will also include the influence which may be the result of the special form which various passages assume. Certain passages, when brought into connection with the keyboard, may on account of its peculiarities be more readily memorized by one form than another. At the same time, however, there are many passages which are suitable to be memorized by several forms—such as Ex. 6, which appeals equally to the musical, visual, or muscular memory—and any final principle should give us some indication of the *one* special form which will be chiefly relied upon in such instances. We may therefore regard the influence derived from the particular form of passages as of an accidental nature, and which may be dismissed from further consideration.

63. We will now pass to our Second possible source of influence—the METHOD EMPLOYED IN STUDYING A PIECE. Here two cases offer themselves for consideration. *First*, the memorization of pieces which lie *within the student's executive powers*. In these cases he repeats the whole or portions simply that he may impress them upon his memory, and the various forms of memory employed would have equal opportunity to assist in the task of memorizing. Their suitability to the task and the relative superiority of them in the individual would probably determine the extent of their employment. Our *Second* case would be the memorization of pieces which are *beyond the student's executive powers*, and which he learns to play and memorize simultaneously. In studying such, he often, in the first instance, concentrates his attention chiefly on acquiring and perfecting the necessary finger movements, and by frequent repetition of such, in order to secure absolute certainty of performance, probably memorizes large portions of the piece by muscular memory, the mere repetition of the movements required bringing that form into employment. Beyond noting that his tone was clear and firm such would not engage much

of his attention. Thus it will be seen that the frequent repetition which is required in order to acquire the power of playing passages, which are relatively speaking, difficult, inevitably forces into employment the muscular memory to a larger extent than would be the case if greater powers of execution were posessed. On the other hand, if to play the correct notes of a passage presents no difficulty, but it presents one in securing the correct gradation and varieties of tone, then our attention would be chiefly directed to listening and criticising the succession of notes and the tone of such, and although the movements would be repeated, and thus to some extent memorized, yet because they present little or no difficulty and consequently receive a smaller amount of attention, the muscular memory would be less secure than the musical one.

64. The special difficulty which a passage presents to a student will be that to the overcoming of which he will direct the greater part of his attention, and the organ of sense chiefly appealed to will be as it were *forced* into employment to a greater extent than other powers, and the passage will tend to be most securely memorized by this form of memory. The influence in the selection of special forms which is exerted by the method of study, varies therefore, it will be seen, according to the difficulties presented by the piece, and we shall have to look still deeper into the matter if any fundamental principle of selection is to be discovered.

65. We have now considered the influence exerted by the music itself, and by the method of studying it; but beyond bringing into prominence the fact that the special nature of music and the necessary conditions of its performance favour the employment of certain powers rather than others, we have discovered no data from which it would be possible to deduce a principle or law admitting of general application, as to the relative extent to which the various forms of memory are employed. We will therefore turn our attention to the Third source of influence arising out of the PECULIARITIES OF THE INDIVIDUAL ENGAGED IN MEMORIZING, for it is clear that if a principle does exist, his personal endowments should supply us with the data from which it must be discovered.

66. Here two distinct aspects claim our attention. The first is the relatively different degrees of retentive power possessed by the various senses employed, as exhibited in the average individual. Thus the eye possesses the greatest power, the ear a lower power, and the muscular memory a power much lower still, while our power of intellectual memory would correspond to our power of general retentiveness. The other aspect of the individual which we have to note is the possession of superior or inferior natural gifts, such as a peculiarly sensitive ear, or eye, or a delicate muscular sense. Beyond recognizing the twofold aspect in which the powers of the individual may be regarded, it will not be necessary to discuss them otherwise than collectively, and with this object we shall therefore turn our attention for a moment from a consideration of the single faculty of memory, and glance at the complete group of powers or faculties, as exhibited by the individual, and the influence which these may have in directing his tastes and pursuits.

67. The pursuits of individuals, when not influenced by outward circumstances or necessity, tend in the direction of their natural aptitudes and abilities   We prefer to do what we can do well, with the least amount of trouble—or what we think we can do well, for a "good performance" is but a relative term. It is only matured judgment, or necessity, which induces us to devote ourselves to what is not only not pleasant, but may be repugnant—often not to what we can do well, but to what pays well. Thus, as a rule, our interests follow the bent of our superior faculties, or our special local endowments. The superiority of any organ of sense, either in its natural condition, or because education and opportunities have given it a more complete development than the others, inevitably carries with it a special interest in the class of sensation with which it is associated, and the development of a memory for corresponding impressions invariably follows. This is a rough and general idea of our intellectual tendencies when left to take their own course. The powers which we possess in a superior degree, unconsciously direct our attention in special directions, and force us to view what is presented to us in a particular light, and therefore to remember it most easily in that aspect. Is it unreasonable to suggest that this kind of natural law supplies the most probable and satisfactory basis for an ultimate principle of selection with regard to the various forms of memory which may be employed upon a passage of piano music?

68. To calculate to any definite extent the amount of assistance supplied by the various forms of memory is quite impossible, yet, after making due allowance for the special nature of music, the requirements of musical performance, the inequalities of the retentive capacities of the powers employed, and the various accidental circumstances which may influence the result, we think the statement of this principle in the following general terms supplies no unsatisfactory solution to the problem under discussion, thus:—*In memorizing piano music we shall employ and rely upon the several forms of memory possible, in a greater or less degree according to the relative superiority of them in us (both natural and acquired), and according as we find the employment of one form easier and more reliable than another.* A kind of instinctive feeling induces us to unconsciously select some forms in preference to others, and we employ that which most readily appears on the scene to help us whenever anything is presented for memorization.

69. The relative superiority of our faculties, to which this principle of selection conforms, will influence us in our manner of regarding passages, and cause individuals to look at the same passage from quite different standpoints. Thus one who has dived deeply into the Theory of Music may view passages in quite another light to one who has but a superficial knowledge of it; and while one with a fine and retentive ear may rely chiefly on musical memory, another who possesses a dull and imperfectly trained ear, although able to say within reasonable limits what a passage *is not*, may by this faculty be unable to supply any further information as to what *it is*. But whichever form of memory we seem to rely most upon, the instances where such was working entirely alone and without assistance from other forms, would be rare and, in many instances, unsafe.

PART II.

THE CULTIVATION OF MUSICAL MEMORY.

CHAPTER VIII.

THE NECESSITY FOR THE CULTIVATION OF MUSICAL MEMORY.

70. The adequate training of the faculty of memory in one or more of its forms, although of varying importance in different branches of education, can in none be regarded as unimportant. The artist must have a trained memory for colours and forms, the linguist for articulate sounds, and of not less importance is it that the musician should have one for musical sounds. To be able to retain and recall at pleasure the sound of the intervals and chords commonly employed in music, is the least we have a right to expect from every musician. From those of higher claims and pretentions we get much more, and among our many gifted living musicians, the possession of wonderful memories is not their least remarkable characteristic.

71. EAR-TRAINING.—The distinguishing feature of a musician should be the possession of a trained ear, and in the words of a previous chapter, this may be said to include three distinct possessions, namely: the ear trained to discriminate different intervals and chords, the memory trained to retain their sound, and the intellect trained to classify them, and to associate the classification with the signs of some form of musical notation. From this it will be seen that what is termed "ear-training," is very largely a cultivation of the memory for musical sounds, and considering the important position which this subject ought to hold, and the inadequate attention it generally receives, in most schemes of musical education, we shall make no apology for devoting some small space to its discussion.

72. It has always seemed to us not a little curious that the characteristic feature of the musician, a trained ear, should have so small an amount of special attention, particularly in the training of keyboard players. Not only is this the case with elementary pupils, amongst whom it is practically ignored, but even amongst pianists who in some respects are proficient executants. Yet that such is a fact is proved every day by the inability of so many of this class *to hear mentally*, with any degree of certainty, what is printed, merely by looking at it—in other words, to *read* music. The power of reading music is analogous to the power of reading ordinary literature, and should not be confused

with the power of "playing at sight," for which the term is frequently loosely applied. It does not necessarily imply the power of performance at all. To read music means to hear mentally the sound of what is printed, just as our ability to read ordinary literature means our understanding the language employed. And as our ability to read a foreign language depends upon our power to recall the meaning of every word, so our ability to read music depends upon our ability to recall the sounds which are represented by the signs before us, or to combine sounds which we have previously stored, into the new forms presented.

73. The immense popularity of the piano, through the medium of which we are able to produce the accurate sounds of what is printed by associating the printed signs with the arrangement of notes on the keyboard, has made the power of reading music not absolutely necessary to the executant, and it has therefore unfortunately become a neglected power. Despite this fact, the possession of it must still be regarded as one of the chief distinguishing features of the musician, and he should be able to read his Bach, and his Beethoven, as the Greek scholar does his Homer, and the German his Schiller. If we then admit that one of the leading departments of musical education is the learning to *read* music— and in order that we may do this, a trained ear is the chief requisite— it seems obvious that from the very first, a certain amount of attention should be devoted to this branch of study, and that in every rational scheme of musical education, no unimportant place should be given to ear-training or a cultivation of the musical memory.

74. THE CORRECT METHOD OF STUDYING HARMONY.—The vital necessity of such a mode of procedure, and a proof of its present neglect, is most obvious when the study of Harmony and those still more advanced studies, which eventually lead to some form of musical composition, are entered upon. No one will deny that all musical studies must appeal to the sense of hearing. Now, if Harmony is one of these, and the one which teaches us how to take correctly our first steps in musical composition—and this we believe it to be—its signs must ever suggest in the mind living sounds, and the moment the exercises become a skilful manipulation on paper of crotchets and quavers, and appeal merely to the understanding and not to the ear, the study loses its true character, and becomes largely a non-musical one, which to some extent might be pursued by the intelligent deaf and dumb. For the student to devote nearly his whole attention to the treatment of chords on paper, without being able to hear mentally what is written down, is the result of a method of harmony-teaching and examining very much in vogue in the present day, and which is in open defiance to that great principle of education which affirms that the *Thing* (in the present instance the *sound*), should be first perceived, and its *Sign* introduced afterwards. Unfortunately, our present method is to emphasize the *sign* at the expense of the *sound*, and to work Harmony exercises after the manner in which we play a game of chess. Our one object is to check-mate our opponent—the so-called teacher—by correctly resolving the discords and avoiding forbidden consecutives. When we have successfully accomplished this, we generally feel some not un-natural desire to hear what our exercise sounds like, and we

forthwith go to the piano to discover its beauties. If our task has been the harmonization of a melody, or any similar exercise which leaves the selection of chords to the pupil, it is curious how rarely a progression which could in any sense be described as beautiful is discoverable. We do not think we are overstating the case when we say that no student discovered what a special gift he possessed for introducing the greatest number of ugly harmonic progressions in the smallest number of bars, until he began to harmonize melodies. The student we do not condemn, but we do not acquit either the method by which he is taught, the teacher who employs the method, or the examiner who connives at its employment by examining harmony students entirely by paper work, and who thereby tends to encourage a radically wrong perception of the subject. The solution of this problem is the *clear memorization of the sound of every chord* as it is introduced for study, and before any but a very general idea of its treatment is given; and to prove this has been done effectually by the ability to write chords and short progressions of such from dictation; as, however, we believe the cure really lies in the hands of musical examiners, we have reserved our final words on this subject until Chapter XII.

75. THE PERFORMANCE OF PIANO MUSIC FROM MEMORY.—Hitherto we have considered the necessity of the cultivation of musical memory quite apart from its connection with performance, we will now endeavour to show the necessity, or at least the advisability, of the cultivation of it (and also of the other forms employed) from the point of view of the executant who is desirous of becoming a fully equipped musician.

76. At the present time all the greatest executants play without the book, and many who are not great, in this respect follow in the train of those they fain would rival, and we cannot but think that every one who is looking forward to public performance, must recognize the fact that memory-playing is no unimportant condition in helping to secure success. But putting aside all thoughts of public performance, simply as a form of mental training, we think all fairly advanced piano students should be taught to play to some extent without the book. Before we teach school boys to recite Shakespeare, we do not inquire whether they are intended for the "Lyceum," or the House of Commons, or for public reciting and speaking of any kind. Their learning to recite from memory is amongst other things a means of training their memory for continued and sustained effort, and as such is a valuable intellectual exercise. If musical education means, not merely gaining a certain facility in performing upon one, or more musical instruments, and a knowledge of Harmony and Counterpoint sufficient to create in us a holy horror of "fifths," and "tritones," but in its true sense embraces a harmonious training and development of all the physical, intellectual and emotional powers employed by the musician, then we see no reason for omitting a course of memory training for sustained effort from the education of the piano student. The neglect with which this power is treated in musical education often leads students to assert that they have no memory for musical performance. The majority of individuals possess the various powers of memory in some degree, but whether they know how to train them, and to exercise

them with the greatest advantage, and thus acquire the security necessary for musical performance, is quite another question.

77. Because, however, we have insisted upon a musician possessing a cultivated memory for musical sounds, and recommended that he should also possess one for musical performance, we hope our readers will not infer that we have any desire to increase the amount of public or semi-public memory-playing which is prevalent at the present day. In fact we do not hesitate to pronounce the fashion, now so universally adopted, of playing without the book, to be one of questionable value, if it is not in some cases absolutely harmful. It is not to those who possess great powers of concentration and retention that any harm can accrue; these doubtless play far better without the assistance of the music, but for those who do not feel their memory absolutely secure, yet whom public opinion, more or less compels to play from memory, the prolonged strain of anxiety and nervousness, in addition to casting its shadow over their performance, exercises, for a considerable period previous to this, no slight or salutary influence upon their bodily and mental health. Despite this, the judicious introduction of memory-playing, simply as a form of training and not for public exhibition, cannot, we think, be without distinct value.

78. In the following chapters we shall offer for our reader's consideration some suggestions with reference to the study of music for memory performance. FIRST, *with regard to the general conditions which favour memorization, drawing attention to their application to the special subject before us;* SECOND, *the principles which should guide us in framing a scheme for training the memory of the piano student;* THIRD, *the method of studying pieces for memorization.*

teaching these the piano, the interest is more readily secured and retained in pieces of a picturesque and suggestive character with suitable titles, than in pieces of a more classical style, such as Etudes and Sonatinas. To overcome the difficulties of the former they will readily give their best efforts, while the latter receive but an unwilling service and a half-hearted devotion. At the same time we must bear in mind that the prettiness of a melody may create a desire to proceed rapidly, and probably carelessly, and this may prevent due attention being given to the finger-movements; but in most five-finger exercises there is little temptation to transfer the interest to the melodic direction; their beauty does not increase—or perhaps it would be more truthful in many cases to say their ugliness does not lessen—as they proceed. This motive to secure concentration—a present performance producing a present pleasure—will also be a powerful one with advanced performers who play music of very different styles, and who will probably feel more in sympathy with some than with others. This is due partly to natural taste, and partly to education. Many enjoy Mendelssohn and Chopin, to whom Bach and Brahms afford no pleasure. Other conditions being the same, the pieces which give us the greatest pleasure to play will be more easily retained than pieces from which we derive less pleasure.

86. A less powerful motive to concentration, yet one which appeals strongly to minds of some maturity, is presented when we are engaged in *an employment which induces pleasure in prospect.* It is this motive of future or prospective good which supports the musical student in his daily practice of technical exercises and the less interesting class of studies.

87. Besides the exercise of our power of concentration for acquisition, the exercise of it continuously and completely for a considerable time is of course necessary for all memory or reproductive performances of any extent.

88. III. REPETITION OF THE IMPRESSION TO BE RETAINED.—The amount of repetition necessary to securely memorize a series of impressions will depend upon the two previous conditions, viz., the power of memory possessed by the individual for the special class of impression, and the degree to which he can concentrate himself. Any deficiency in these must be compensated for by additional repetition. At the same time it must not be overlooked that, in the average individual, the different senses possess the power of memory in very unequal degrees. The Visual memory is in general the strongest power, then comes the Auditory, and in a lower position the Muscular memory. One presentation might be sufficient for either of the former, but would be wholly inadequate for the latter.

89. The consideration of these general conditions has naturally proceeded on lines very similar to their exposition in other works on Memory, but while it is admitted that they may be found in every text-book on the subject, any text-book like the present in which they were omitted, and the reader's attention not drawn to their special application, would be incomplete.

CHAPTER X.

SOME SUGGESTIONS FOR A SCHEME OF MEMORY TRAINING.

90. We shall now endeavour to show the application of some of the general principles which underlie any course of memory training to the special needs and studies of the piano student.

91. STATE OF ADVANCEMENT NECESSARY.—Before the question of memory-playing is presented to the pupil, all the different departments of piano-playing—the training of the hand and fingers to move with facility and certainty, the ear to criticise both correctness of notes, rhythm, and gradation of tone, and the power of reading music with some degree of fluency—all should be in a moderate state of advancement, otherwise the attention may be withdrawn from vital matters which are insecure, and directed towards that which, at this stage of advancement, is not of the greatest moment, even if in some cases desirable. Playing from memory is an *ultimate* condition of performance and can never be advanced as an excuse for any remissness in the rendering of a piece. The teacher must decide for each individual pupil when it can be safely introduced, and every competent teacher will know that to some pupils whose practice is little, whose progress is less, and whose musical intelligence is nil, it should never be introduced at all.

92. THE VALUE OF EARLY TRAINING.—Psychologists tell us that the natural power of memory is greatest between the ages of 9 and 14, and after the latter age it gradually becomes less. The greater ease with which in after life we appear to make new acquisitions is ostensible, and not real, our extended knowledge prevents anything from being absolutely new to us, and few subjects which we attack have not many vital associations and connections with our present knowledge. This is not less true with regard to music. Many are able to employ and rely upon their memory for musical performance, in mature years, with a greater ease and security, and to a far larger extent than was possible for them to do when they were quite young. This is partly due to training and exercise, but also partly due to the employment of Intellectual memory in connection with music, and regarding and memorizing music in an aspect which appeals but in a small degree to those of an early age, even if it is presented to them. We must not, however, be understood to minimise the importance of teaching young pianists of sufficient advancement to play from memory, especially if such are looking forward to careers as public performers. The security which the habit of memory-playing formed in youth gives, and the power of continuous concentration thus acquired, can rarely be developed to an equal degree when such efforts are not attempted until mature years are reached.

forthwith go to the piano to discover its beauties. If our task has been the harmonization of a melody, or any similar exercise which leaves the selection of chords to the pupil, it is curious how rarely a progression which could in any sense be described as beautiful is discoverable. We do not think we are overstating the case when we say that no student discovered what a special gift he possessed for introducing the greatest number of ugly harmonic progressions in the smallest number of bars, until he began to harmonize melodies. The student we do not condemn, but we do not acquit either the method by which he is taught, the teacher who employs the method, or the examiner who connives at its employment by examining harmony students entirely by paper work, and who thereby tends to encourage a radically wrong perception of the subject. The solution of this problem is the *clear memorization of the sound of every chord* as it is introduced for study, and before any but a very general idea of its treatment is given; and to prove this has been done effectually by the ability to write chords and short progressions of such from dictation; as, however, we believe the cure really lies in the hands of musical examiners, we have reserved our final words on this subject until Chapter XII.

75. THE PERFORMANCE OF PIANO MUSIC FROM MEMORY.—Hitherto we have considered the necessity of the cultivation of musical memory quite apart from its connection with performance, we will now endeavour to show the necessity, or at least the advisability, of the cultivation of it (and also of the other forms employed) from the point of view of the executant who is desirous of becoming a fully equipped musician.

76. At the present time all the greatest executants play without the book, and many who are not great, in this respect follow in the train of those they fain would rival, and we cannot but think that every one who is looking forward to public performance, must recognize the fact that memory-playing is no unimportant condition in helping to secure success. But putting aside all thoughts of public performance, simply as a form of mental training, we think all fairly advanced piano students should be taught to play to some extent without the book. Before we teach school boys to recite Shakespeare, we do not inquire whether they are intended for the "Lyceum," or the House of Commons, or for public reciting and speaking of any kind. Their learning to recite from memory is amongst other things a means of training their memory for continued and sustained effort, and as such is a valuable intellectual exercise. If musical education means, not merely gaining a certain facility in performing upon one, or more musical instruments, and a knowledge of Harmony and Counterpoint sufficient to create in us a holy horror of "fifths," and "tritones," but in its true sense embraces a harmonious training and development of all the physical, intellectual and emotional powers employed by the musician, then we see no reason for omitting a course of memory training for sustained effort from the education of the piano student. The neglect with which this power is treated in musical education often leads students to assert that they have no memory for musical performance. The majority of individuals possess the various powers of memory in some degree, but whether they know how to train them, and to exercise

them with the greatest advantage, and thus acquire the security necessary for musical performance, is quite another question.

77. Because, however, we have insisted upon a musician possessing a cultivated memory for musical sounds, and recommended that he should also possess one for musical performance, we hope our readers will not infer that we have any desire to increase the amount of public or semi-public memory-playing which is prevalent at the present day. In fact we do not hesitate to pronounce the fashion, now so universally adopted, of playing without the book, to be one of questionable value, if it is not in some cases absolutely harmful. It is not to those who possess great powers of concentration and retention that any harm can accrue; these doubtless play far better without the assistance of the music, but for those who do not feel their memory absolutely secure, yet whom public opinion, more or less compels to play from memory, the prolonged strain of anxiety and nervousness, in addition to casting its shadow over their performance, exercises, for a considerable period previous to this, no slight or salutary influence upon their bodily and mental health. Despite this, the judicious introduction of memory-playing, simply as a form of training and not for public exhibition, cannot, we think, be without distinct value.

78. In the following chapters we shall offer for our reader's consideration some suggestions with reference to the study of music for memory performance. FIRST, *with regard to the general conditions which favour memorization, drawing attention to their application to the special subject before us;* SECOND, *the principles which should guide us in framing a scheme for training the memory of the piano student;* THIRD, *the method of studying pieces for memorization.*

CHAPTER IX.

GENERAL CONDITIONS FAVOURABLE TO MEMORIZING.

79. In the present chapter we shall consider quite briefly the conditions which are favourable to acquisition or memorizing in any form, and show some of the special applications of these to the particular subject before us, the memorization of piano music.

80. In general education the memorizing of new materials is the operation requiring the greatest expenditure of mental vigour. In applying this statement to the memorizing of piano music, we may have to modify it somewhat in the letter, although not in the spirit. The memorizing of new pieces by the piano student, can hardly be said to exactly correspond with the learning of a number of unknown words by the student of Latin or Greek. To the fairly advanced and intelligent pianist who knows something of Harmony, a new piece is often but a presentation of old materials in a fresh aspect, or in a new construction, rather than the introduction of absolutely new matter, at least to any very great extent. Considering the immense amount of really fine and original music which exists, the very limited amount of material from which it is evolved is one of the most remarkable facts connected with the Art. Again, in studying a piano piece, our first efforts are generally directed towards acquiring the power to play it; and if its technical difficulties are sufficient to require us to repeat some passages many times over, we shall probably memorize these by muscular memory whilst we are learning to play them, if not also by other forms as well; the two operations of improving the powers of execution, and of memorizing, frequently proceeding simultaneously. The task, therefore, which may be said to make the greatest demand upon the mental power of the piano-student will be the studying of a new piece (with the object of ultimately performing it from memory), which not only presents technical difficulties to him, but which presents an aspect of musical materials with which he is unfamiliar, and a mode of construction upon a higher intellectual basis than that of his previous studies. To turn our attention to a mature work by Beethoven or Schumann, after studying works say by Mendelssohn, would illustrate this transition to a higher plane of thought and conception; and such a task should be undertaken when mind and body are quite fresh. Mental operations, in which the intellect is interpreting a new style and the memory is receiving new impressions, cannot be successfully undertaken when the nervous powers are at a low ebb.

81. For recalling and reproducing the storages of previous occasions a similar mental and physical condition is not so vital, and it is not unusual to see in schemes for practice-time, suggested in pianoforte

primers, the concluding portion allotted to playing from memory, yet the fresher we are, the more successful and complete will be our efforts in this direction. Failure in such may be due, not to insufficient or imperfect ingraining, but to a low state of nervous force at our command when we wish to revive previous acquisitions.

82. Beyond the general condition of mind and body there are three special conditions upon which the success of memorizing depends. These are (1) degree of retentiveness peculiar to the individual, (2) power of concentration possessed by him, (3) repetition of the impression to be retained.

83. I. DEGREE OF RETENTIVENESS PECULIAR TO THE INDIVIDUAL.—This refers to the power of memory bestowed upon us by nature, and which, according to the latest theories of Psychologists, is a limited quantity in each individual—special memories, such as those for colours, sounds, etc., varying *directly* as the discriminative power of the organ employed. By continuous and judicious exercise our various forms of memory may be developed to their fullest extent, yet there is a limit beyond which we cannot go; and no form can be said to be unlimited in capacity. Such being the case, the importance of economising the power we possess, and regarding everything in its simplest aspect, is obvious. Our aim should be to remember passages and complete movements by that method which will reduce our mental labour to a minimum. In the common things of life, and in the study of the Sciences, this end is obtained by generalisation and classification, and what we have termed the Intellectual aspect of music is simply an application of the same principles to its material.

84. II. POWER OF CONCENTRATION POSSESSED BY THE INDIVIDUAL.—To concentrate ourselves upon any subject, or to give our whole mind and attention to any work we may be engaged upon, is the most rapid and successful means of accomplishing and mastering it. If our occupation be some form of memorizing, the ability to direct all our powers towards this one object is an immense help to us; in fact the acquirement of this power of voluntary concentration is one of the chief ends of education. Although the exercise of this power depends very largely upon an effort of the Will, yet the assistance to be secured by a co-operation of the Feelings is an invaluable one, and indispensable in early training. We give our attention most readily and most completely to those employments of which the simple performance affords us pleasure, or for which we have a natural taste. As explained in our first chapter, a taste for anything is generally the result of the possession of a corresponding superior natural organ, which by its special sensibility brings a particular form of sensation prominently before the mind, and the exercise of any organ which we possess in a superior degree, always affords us a certain amount of pleasure. *Thus the greatest motive to concentration, a present employment inducing a present pleasure, is presented when our employment brings into play our superior natural organs, or in other words, when it coincides with our natural tastes.*

85. With children and those possessing immature minds generally, this is by far the most efficient means of securing the attention. When

teaching these the piano, the interest is more readily secured and retained in pieces of a picturesque and suggestive character with suitable titles, than in pieces of a more classical style, such as Etudes and Sonatinas. To overcome the difficulties of the former they will readily give their best efforts, while the latter receive but an unwilling service and a half-hearted devotion. At the same time we must bear in mind that the prettiness of a melody may create a desire to proceed rapidly, and probably carelessly, and this may prevent due attention being given to the finger-movements; but in most five-finger exercises there is little temptation to transfer the interest to the melodic direction; their beauty does not increase—or perhaps it would be more truthful in many cases to say their ugliness does not lessen—as they proceed. This motive to secure concentration—a present performance producing a present pleasure—will also be a powerful one with advanced performers who play music of very different styles, and who will probably feel more in sympathy with some than with others. This is due partly to natural taste, and partly to education. Many enjoy Mendelssohn and Chopin, to whom Bach and Brahms afford no pleasure. Other conditions being the same, the pieces which give us the greatest pleasure to play will be more easily retained than pieces from which we derive less pleasure.

86. A less powerful motive to concentration, yet one which appeals strongly to minds of some maturity, is presented when we are engaged in *an employment which induces pleasure in prospect*. It is this motive of future or prospective good which supports the musical student in his daily practice of technical exercises and the less interesting class of studies.

87. Besides the exercise of our power of concentration for acquisition, the exercise of it continuously and completely for a considerable time is of course necessary for all memory or reproductive performances of any extent.

88. III. REPETITION OF THE IMPRESSION TO BE RETAINED.—The amount of repetition necessary to securely memorize a series of impressions will depend upon the two previous conditions, viz., the power of memory possessed by the individual for the special class of impression, and the degree to which he can concentrate himself. Any deficiency in these must be compensated for by additional repetition. At the same time it must not be overlooked that, in the average individual, the different senses possess the power of memory in very unequal degrees. The Visual memory is in general the strongest power, then comes the Auditory, and in a lower position the Muscular memory. One presentation might be sufficient for either of the former, but would be wholly inadequate for the latter.

89. The consideration of these general conditions has naturally proceeded on lines very similar to their exposition in other works on Memory, but while it is admitted that they may be found in every text-book on the subject, any text-book like the present in which they were omitted, and the reader's attention not drawn to their special application, would be incomplete.

CHAPTER X.

SOME SUGGESTIONS FOR A SCHEME OF MEMORY TRAINING.

90. We shall now endeavour to show the application of some of the general principles which underlie any course of memory training to the special needs and studies of the piano student.

91. STATE OF ADVANCEMENT NECESSARY.—Before the question of memory-playing is presented to the pupil, all the different departments of piano-playing—the training of the hand and fingers to move with facility and certainty, the ear to criticise both correctness of notes, rhythm, and gradation of tone, and the power of reading music with some degree of fluency—all should be in a moderate state of advancement, otherwise the attention may be withdrawn from vital matters which are insecure, and directed towards that which, at this stage of advancement, is not of the greatest moment, even if in some cases desirable. Playing from memory is an *ultimate* condition of performance and can never be advanced as an excuse for any remissness in the rendering of a piece. The teacher must decide for each individual pupil when it can be safely introduced, and every competent teacher will know that to some pupils whose practice is little, whose progress is less, and whose musical intelligence is nil, it should never be introduced at all.

92. THE VALUE OF EARLY TRAINING.—Psychologists tell us that the natural power of memory is greatest between the ages of 9 and 14, and after the latter age it gradually becomes less. The greater ease with which in after life we appear to make new acquisitions is ostensible, and not real, our extended knowledge prevents anything from being absolutely new to us, and few subjects which we attack have not many vital associations and connections with our present knowledge. This is not less true with regard to music. Many are able to employ and rely upon their memory for musical performance, in mature years, with a greater ease and security, and to a far larger extent than was possible for them to do when they were quite young. This is partly due to training and exercise, but also partly due to the employment of Intellectual memory in connection with music, and regarding and memorizing music in an aspect which appeals but in a small degree to those of an early age, even if it is presented to them. We must not, however, be understood to minimise the importance of teaching young pianists of sufficient advancement to play from memory, especially if such are looking forward to careers as public performers. The security which the habit of memory-playing formed in youth gives, and the power of continuous concentration thus acquired, can rarely be developed to an equal degree when such efforts are not attempted until mature years are reached.

93. PRINCIPLES WHICH SHOULD GUIDE US IN THE SELECTION OF PIECES.—When the powers of execution and general musical knowledge and intelligence of the pupil are sufficiently advanced to warrant our bringing the question of memory-playing before him, our next consideration is what should influence us in selecting pieces for memorization. Such selection should naturally progress from short and simply constructed pieces, to long and difficult ones. It is we believe due to a disregard of this, to us, most obvious condition of training, that the inability of many excellent pianists to play from memory is due. Playing without the book is frequently not attempted until a high degree of execution is reached, when pieces both lengthy and difficult are studied, and the student's first efforts are often directed to the attempt to memorize such pieces, viz., those of his daily practice. The result is often failure, and he instantly decides that he has no memory for musical performance. He forgets that his powers of execution and understanding have arrived at the stage of advancement sufficient to grapple with the difficulties of these pieces only after years of gradual progress, yet he expects his memory to make the step in one bound. When judiciously trained and regularly exercised, the memory may develop sufficiently to meet the constantly increasing demands made upon it by the increasing power of execution acquired, but such is not necessarily the case. There are many excellent pianists who have trained memories, and who habitually play to some extent from memory, but who do not trust themselves to play without a book pieces which they consider beyond their powers of memory.

94. A progressive training, then, as is required for the development of all the other powers, is also a vital condition for developing the memory to its fullest extent. In early attempts the chief object should be to isolate the difficulty of memorizing, and to eliminate as far as possible all other difficulties, that is, to select pieces well within the executive and interpretative powers of the pupil. Something which has been learnt and put aside for a time is often useful to begin with, as in such pieces not only have the technical difficulties been conquered, but a good general idea of the piece is probably retained.

95. Putting aside the question of the memorization of past pieces, our selection should be guided by the following conditions, the qualification of which, as to shortness and simplicity, being regarded as relative to the powers of the pupil. The pieces should be—*First*, Short in length; *Second*, Simple in form and construction; *Third*, Simple in detail; *Fourth*, Moderate in difficulty.

96. (I.) The first, *Short in length*, hardly needs comment. It is an obvious condition of all early sustained effort, and how far it will limit such will depend on the natural strength of the memory, and upon the power possessed of continuous concentration for the purposes of reproduction. Successful public reciters and speakers, as well as public performers, must possess both of these powers in a high degree. The pianist may have to begin his memory playing with the shortest of Mendelssohn's "Lieder," but after regular exercise and continually increasing effort he may not stop until he has reached Beethoven's longest Concerto.

97. (II.) *Simplicity in Form and Construction* is a condition which demands fuller consideration.

The simplest form which intelligible musical thought assumes, is that of an air or melody, and the simplest form employed in piano music is an accompanied melody. Pieces of this class, possessing one melodic idea with a simple harmonic accompaniment which merely colours and supports the melody, and does not introduce any special features of a new melodic or rhythmic nature, are the easiest to remember. Directly we introduce in combination with our chief melodic idea, others, either melodic or rhythmic, of a contrasted nature, and thus increase the interest and importance of our accompanying matter, we add to the complexity of what is to be memorized, and therefore increase the difficulty of memorizing. Music which answers to this description, while being built upon a harmonic foundation, is often both poly-melodic and poly-rhythmic in character. As it increases in complexity, so the memorizing of it increases in difficulty, until we reach the most difficult style of all to memorize—contrapuntal music, where every part is of equal importance and difficulty. Thus, disregarding any sympathy we may have for one style rather than another, our extremes of simplicity and difficulty are represented respectively by simple harmonic construction and pure contrapuntal construction. The greater portion of piano music lies somewhere between these two, and while being harmonic in structure, exhibits a combination of different melodies and rhythms which is of the essence, if not the actual form of contrapuntal music.

98. It is impossible to indicate any definite boundary lines between the different styles, but as a broad principle we may say, that the more brilliant and less intellectual a composition is, the more does its construction tend towards a simple rather than a complex harmonic structure. There is less material employed, and therefore it is easier to memorize. Thus the music of composers such as Mendelssohn and Weber, is as a general rule easier to remember than that of Beethoven, Schumann, and Brahms, while these again are simpler than Bach. This classification will not of course apply to every piece by these composers. There are pieces by Bach which are easier to remember than some of the piano fugues of Mendelssohn, but the general style of the majority of their works has guided us in placing them in this order, and suggestions as to general lines of study is all we presume to offer.

99. (III.) *Simplicity in Detail.*—It is most important that we should learn every piece thoroughly from the book before attempting to memorize it as a whole, in order that we may note every detail with regard to phrasing and expression, as well as to notes and rhythm. Unless we are complete masters of such details when the book is before us, they will certainly fare badly when we have the additional task of remembering them. In our early efforts, if we are not most watchful, the extra demand made upon us when playing without the book will tend to make other things suffer, and perhaps what may be rendered in-correctly and most easily pass unnoticed, is bad phrasing and expression. Our first efforts, therefore, should be directed to pieces which are not characterized by too great a wealth of detail of this description. Here,

again, as a general rule, the works of Mendelssohn make less demand upon us than those of Beethoven, and many of Beethoven's less than those of Chopin and Schumann. Until our memory is quite reliable for pieces which are simple both in construction and detail, it is unwise to attempt pieces of a more complex and intricate nature.

100. (IV.) Our last condition is *Moderate in Difficulty.*—In order to give an adequate interpretation of a work from the book, it is necessary that all its technical difficulties should be well within our powers, and this condition should be still more emphasised if to the difficulty of performance we add the extra effort of playing from memory. It is idle to pretend that we are in any sense interpreting a piece, if, whether we are playing from the book or not, all our powers are employed in overcoming its technical difficulties.

101. As previously stated the qualifications of these conditions are purely relative to the powers of the pupil, and the extent to which they apply to any special piece must be decided by the teacher, or if the student has not the guidance of such, he must experiment with his own powers, and decrease his test pieces in length and difficulty, until he has discovered the degree to which he can securely memorize, even if it be but the shortest and simplest of Mendelssohn's "Lieder." Upon such a foundation he must gradually build, ever remembering that only by regular daily exercise and constant effort to remember pieces of greater length and difficulty, will he fully develop his retentive powers and make them thoroughly reliable and secure.

CHAPTER XI.

A METHOD OF STUDYING PIECES FOR MEMORIZATION.

102. Before proceeding to the ultimate condition of the performance of a piece, that of memorizing it in its entirety, in addition to the power of playing it with accuracy and suitable expression, a thoroughly intelligent understanding of it should be acquired. By this we mean a recognition of its leading themes, the order of their occurrence, and the relationship of the keys in which they appear, also, if there be a wealth of elaboration which prevents one from perceiving readily the form of the themes or the order of some of the progressions; the outlines of such themes or such progressions, should be written out by the pupil. No earnest student will regard these demands as unreasonable, and when complied with, they will form a solid, mental foundation upon which he can safely and gradually graft all the details of a piece in correct order.

103. In many compositions, especially those in sonata-form, there is a large amount of recapitulation and repetition, and passages frequently occur which, while resembling one another in the main, differ in small yet not unimportant details. In such passages, unless the points of difference are clearly brought before the mind of the student, are carefully compared, and specially memorized, such details may possibly suffer. We will therefore lead the student through the first movement of Beethoven's First Sonata, showing him how such may be analysed, and drawing his attention to points of interest in the structure and methods employed, as well as to other features which may help him towards the accurate memorization of it. It will be seen that by so doing we can appeal only to the Intellectual memory. In the other forms, repetition is the chief means of bringing such into employment, but in regarding a piece Intellectually we bring to our assistance previously acquired knowledge of the theory of music and musical composition. How far a student needs, or can employ the suggestions given, each must judge for himself.

MUSICAL MEMORY.

BEETHOVEN, Op. 2, No. 1.

MUSICAL MEMORY. 57

104. *Analysis of the First movement of Beethoven's Sonata, Op. 2, No. 1.*—This movement is in regular sonata-form; the key is F minor, and the second subject is in A flat. Our broadest idea of it, therefore, would be thus:—

Key F minor.	Key A flat.	Development.	Key F minor.	Key F minor.
1st Subject.	2nd Subject		1st Subject.	2nd Subject.

Now let us examine it more closely. The First Subject (8 bars) is, with the exception of one chord, founded entirely upon Tonic and Dominant harmonies. The bass with its *stepwise* progression from the Tonic to the Dominant should be noticed. The first phrase of the first subject is now introduced in the bass in C minor (b. 9, 10), but the immediate introduction of D flat (b. 11) induces a modulation to the key of A flat, the dominant chord of which key is shortly reached (b. 16). The emphasizing of the cadence to the chord of E flat by *three* occurrences of the same progression, further intensified at each repetition (b. 15-20) should be noticed. The Second Subject, in A flat, now appears (b. 21), and is a phrase of two bars, which, like the last one referred to, is heard *three* times. The third time it is incomplete, and passes at once into a figure of *changing-notes* which progress upward, while the part for the left hand takes a downward direction. The passage culminates eventually in a descending scale passage with a syncopated bass part (b. 33-36); these four bars are repeated with the bass part an octave lower, the upper part having a different initial note and an altered ending. The form and progression of the cadence-figure (b. 41-3), a phrase of two bars which is also heard *three* times, is quite simple.

105. The study of the DEVELOPMENT is in every way interesting, and considering the early Opus number of the work to which it belongs (Op. 2), it reveals in a remarkable manner the germ of several of Beethoven's most characteristic "methods," which are only shown in their maturity in much later works. We shall therefore discuss it somewhat fully. First, we notice that the two subjects are developed in their regular order; and then, the importance which is given to the Second Subject. Both of these methods of procedure are exceptional with Beethoven. The first special Beethoven device is the new form of the First Subject, which is introduced in phrases of three bars instead of two. Another is the regular order in the progression of the keys. Thus this portion starts with the first subject in A flat major, modulates to B flat minor, introducing the Second Subject in that key (b. 56), and thence on to C minor (b. 63), from whence it returns through B flat minor (b 70), to A flat (b. 72), and proceeds to the Dominant Chord of F minor (b. 77). In the passage immediately preceding the Dominant Pedal C (b. 81), leading to the Recapitulation, we must draw attention to another favourite device of Beethoven. Often after he has reached his goal, in this case C, the Dominant of F minor, he immediately quits it and returns to it again in a more emphatic and forcible manner. Thus

the bass first progresses, B flat, C (b. 76, 77), but secondly, B flat, B natural, C (b. 79 to 81). We have now reached the dominant of the original key leading directly back to the Recapitulation. The manner in which Beethoven habitually emphasises this point, and thus intensifies our longing for the return of the original key and first subject, is well-known to every Beethoven student, and the fact that out of a development of 52 bars, 20 are occupied in circling around this dominant, and preparing the mind to welcome with ever increasing eagerness the return of the tonic, shows again how remarkably this early Sonata reveals, in no uncertain manner, a device which we only see fully developed in the greatest works of this composer. Even over this pedal the emotions of the listener are more and more excited by a skilful and subtle method of increasing elaboration.

106. We have now reached the RECAPITULATION, and, quite apart from the manner in which it differs in general structure from the first portion, we must carefully note the points in which it may differ, but to the smallest extent, from the earlier version of the corresponding passages. Such, if not carefully compared, are liable to suffer when played from memory. The first difference we detect is in the bass of bars 105 to 108, where the entry, taking place on the accented instead of the unaccented beats of the bar, gives a fresh interest to the passage. After the pause, the re-entry on the chord of F minor instead of C minor must be carefully noted. With the exception of the presentation of the phrases of the Second Subject in different octaves, there is nothing which requires special comment until we reach the descending scale passage in quavers (b. 132). Here, with the exception of the initial note C, which is the same in both occurrences, the first part of these passages is a reproduction of the corresponding passages in the first portion, and they are not transposed throughout like the bass. The manner in which they end should also be noticed. The cadence-figure (b. 140-2) is harmonized somewhat differently from what it was in the first portion, and there is no small initial note on its first two presentations, otherwise it is repeated the same number of times (three), and then extended into a short coda by means of a harmonic sequence.

107. We have concluded our analysis, and some may think it more suited for a composition student than a piano student, yet it is only by looking deeply into such points that they become indelibly fixed in our memory, and we thus obtain a security in memory-playing which would be difficult to obtain by other methods. Quite apart however from any desire to play from memory, it is only by such a careful and critical study of the works of Beethoven that we become impressed with his wonderful greatness, and this, besides creating in us a deeper interest in his works, should make our interpretation of them, if not perhaps worthy, yet as a result of our earnest efforts to more fully understand him, less unworthy of his unrivalled genius.

108. THE MEMORIZING OF CONCERTOS.[*]—The study of the foregoing analysis will give the student some idea of the methods he may adopt in memorizing most solo piano music, but a few additional words with

---

[*] For the contents of this paragraph I am indebted to Miss Bessie Fédarb. (See Preface.)

special reference to works for piano and orchestra may not be without value. In studying Concertos and similar works in which the piano-part supplies but a fragmentary and incomplete idea of the whole, after the technical difficulties have been to some extent mastered, a clear, general idea of each movement should be obtained. This may be secured, either by having the *tuttis*, or passages for the orchestra alone, supplied on a second piano, or if such is unavailable, by the soloist himself filling up the intervals between the solos on his own instrument. Eventually, when memorizing the work as a whole, the tune of the *tuttis* should be carefully learnt, so that the soloist can in time rehearse the concerto in its entirety by playing merely the solo portions, and when these cease, *mentally* rehearsing the orchestral portions in their correct *tempo*, until the solo instrument re-enters. To possess a detailed idea of the complete work, and the relationship which the piano-part bears to the orchestral-part throughout, as well as the ability to supply on the piano some general idea of the orchestral *tuttis*, is the minimum of knowledge which could produce an intelligent interpretation.

109. REHEARSING FROM MEMORY.—After having successfully memorized a piece, the frequent rehearsal of it tends to make our impression of it more permanent, although the student must carefully guard against any looseness of rhythm or carelessness of phrasing which may possibly result if such rehearsals invariably take place without reference to the book. One eminent teacher recommends his pupils *never to play a piece more than two or three times from memory without returning to the book, to see that they are not departing from its instructions*, and also when rehearsing to have the printed copy near them, so that in the event of any momentary failure of memory, or any uncertainty as to the exact version of a passage, they can instantly refer to it, and by so doing impress it more deeply upon the memory. Such advice cannot be too highly valued or too carefully followed by the average pianist.

110. MENTAL REHEARSAL.—Quite distinct from the method of rehearsing a piece at the piano is the method of mentally rehearsing it, that is, of thinking it carefully through away from the instrument. To do this successfully requires not merely a greater degree of concentration but a reliance on forms of memory other than Muscular memory, which, when rehearsing at the instrument we may unconsciously rely upon to an extent that is unsafe unless other forms are able to rigorously control it. Passages which resemble one another as wholes but differ in details, as Ex. 11, or which begin alike but lead in different directions, as Ex. 22, are only absolutely secure if they can be accurately rehearsed away from the instrument.

CHAPTER XII.

MEMORY TRAINING AND EXAMINATION SCHEMES.

111. Few we think will care to deny, that in the present day, the education of the musical student, while ostensibly in the hands of the teacher, is really directed and controlled by those who frame the many schemes of examination which now exist. In fact the large majority of pupils make no secret of their desire to secure some certificate, diploma, or degree which shall testify to their ability in one or more departments of musical study.

112. THE INFLUENCE OF EXAMINATIONS.—If it were certain that every examination scheme before the public was framed by musicians who were thoroughly able musical educationalists in the broadest sense of the term, that is, not merely teachers in some one or two special departments, but men who realise what is fundamental in any efficient and complete scheme of musical education, as well as the relative importance of the various subjects—musicians who were alive to the immense power they wield for good or for evil in shaping the musical present and future of this country, and were unanimously agreed in demanding a reasonably high standard of efficiency before granting any certificate—the present craze to be examined could do little permanent harm. Unhappily, however, these conditions are very far from being fulfilled at the present time. Perhaps the saddest aspect of the case is presented by the active existence of numerous irresponsible examining bodies, whose methods belong rather to the shop and the market-place than to the practice of a high and honourable profession. Into the nets of these institutions the unwary student, unable to distinguish the true from the false, strays, only however to discover, when it is too late, that he has parted with his substance in return for a most unsatisfactory shadow. But putting this evil—and it is no small or insignificant one—aside, and assuming the atmosphere to be cleared of all these will-o'-the-wisp institutions, there remains yet much to be said against, and much to be laid at the door of the existing state of *over-examination*, for we can describe it in no other words. Whilst loyally acknowledging the large amount of good which has undoubtedly resulted from the establishment of some of the existing boards of examination,* we cannot close our eyes to the fact that the prevailing fashion is responsible for a very large amount of mis-directed, and therefore wasted effort on the part of the musical student. In many ways it has been a serious

---

* In raising the ideal and defining the aims of the teacher, the establishment of the Associated Board of the R.A.M. and R.C.M. may be said to have marked an epoch in Local Examinations in Music.

hindrance to the study of Music for the love of Music itself; it has kindled in us an ambition to become successful candidates or gold and silver medalists, rather than artists and musicians : and it has made us prone to glory in the number and rarity of our alphabetical distinctions rather than that we are apostles of Joy, and high priests of the Beautiful in the glorious Temple of Musical Art.

113. It is not our province to discuss the question of Examinations as a whole, but it was necessary to point out that musical education is practically controlled at the present time by examinations, to show that any weak points in the prevailing scheme of education could be most effectively and completely remedied by modifying our scheme of examination accordingly.

114. THE NECESSITY OF EAR TESTS IN ALL HARMONY EXAMINATIONS. —As we stated in a previous chapter, if there is one specially weak spot in our general scheme of musical education, it is in providing insufficient direct ear-training, or in imperfectly cultivating our memory for musical sounds. We drew attention to the fact that all real progress in Harmony and kindred studies is impossible where such is neglected to any great extent. Considering this, it seems to us little short of fabulous that in recent years, examiners, eminent and experienced, having stood on platforms of associations and examining colleges, and in diploma-distributing and other speeches, having delivered themselves of these same sentiments, having emphasised the importance of ear-training, having asserted that by its neglect other studies suffer, and because it is neglected, harmony students, unable to hear mentally what they write down, manufacture progressions, unsurpassed and unsurpassable in ugliness and absurdity, examiners having stated all this, and thus correctly diagnosed the case, there stop short and fail to take the one step which shall remedy this evil, or to apply the one cure which shall deliver us from the effects of this rampant disease.

115. We must admit that to us the remedy seems as simple as it is obvious. *It consists in compelling students to memorize the sound of intervals, chords, and progressions, and to associate such with their correct signs in musical notation, and to prove that this has been done effectually by their ability to write them down from dictation ; a test in which of some kind should be included in every examination scheme.* We should be wanting in any sense of justice if we here failed to acknowledge the work in this direction done by several examining institutions.* But in the examinations for the diplomas most sought after by professional musicians, we have failed to discover that any dictation tests exist, and yet it is with respect to these higher examinations that complaints of badly harmonized melodies and such like are frequently heard.

116. As a general rule Harmony examinations consist entirely of paper work, yet when we ask students to write harmonic progressions

---

* We here refer to the Tonic Sol-fa College Examinations, and in more recent years and to a limited extent by the Incorporated Society of Musicians, whilst the examinations of the recently established Incorporated Staff Sight Singing College show an advance in this direction of which at present it is impossible to estimate the influence. We are also glad to note that in future, a simple ear-test will be included in the "Practical" Local Examinations held by Trinity College, London.

and harmonize melodies on paper, if it is an examination in *Music* and not an examination merely in the skilful arrangement of the signs of musical notation, we have the right to demand that they *shall* be able to hear mentally what they write down. Now, as examiners are constantly coming forward and stating that, from the papers worked, they are quite confident the majority of candidates do *not* hear what they have written, it is the duty of examiners to alter their scheme which they themselves admit produces such unsatisfactory results, and by the universal introduction of dictation-tests, compel students to give adequate attention to ear-training. No musical examination can be divorced from Music, and MUSIC IS SOUND, NOT PEN AND INK SKETCHES, this must be obvious to the most unintelligent; and if by our present methods we do not get sound, or the proofs of it, it shows our present method, is, if not totally wrong, wrong in so far that what is of primary importance is ignored and what is secondary takes the place of honour. Every Harmony examination therefore should consist of two parts. *First*, the writing of melodies and chords from dictation ; *Second*, the treatment of such on paper. The chords dictated should be of equal advancement with those treated on paper, and a certain percentage of marks for each form of test should be necessary to secure a pass.

117. Such a radical change in our method of examining would require gradual and judicious introduction, but we think the results would rapidly prove that it was the right and complete method, as the unsatisfactory results have conclusively proved that our present method, in so far as it is incomplete, is wrong.

118. MEMORY PERFORMANCES IN EXAMINATIONS.—A brief consideration of memory playing in examination schemes is all that is now necessary to complete our task.

If it is, and we believe it is, a valuable yet neglected part of the training of the pianist, that he should be taught to play without the book, it seems but right that examination schemes, or at least those for the granting of high professional diplomas in solo-playing, should require memory playing to some extent. It seems somewhat of an anomaly that in the competitive examination for scholarships at some of our music schools, the candidates are asked to play from memory, while in the examinations for diplomas granted to these same scholars, when leaving after several years of study, memory-playing beyond that of technical exercises is not required. Surely, if it is expected as a sign of musical intelligence, it may reasonably be demanded when a high degree of training and proficiency is certified to.

CHAPTER XIII.

THE MEMORIES OF MUSICIANS.

119. The present chapter is the result of our efforts to collect from various sources, evidences of the possession of exceptional powers of memory by musicians. As, however, no object would be gained by chronicling the usual type of memory-performance so common at the present time, we have deemed it desirable to place on record only those facts about memory-performances which, on account of their exceptional nature, are of permanent interest, and for this reason the names of many great musicians are omitted, not necessarily because of any deficiency on their part, but because nothing of unusual interest respecting their performances has come to our knowledge.

120. Amongst the most famous feats of memory, and at the time of its performance the most remarkable was that performed by MOZART in connection with Allegri's Miserere in 1770. Mozart and his father were on an Italian tour, and, according to Otto Jahn, "they arrived in Rome about midday on Wednesday in Holy Week amidst a storm of thunder and lightning, 'received like grand people with a discharge of artillery.' There was just time to hurry to the Sistine Chapel and hear Allegri's Miserere. It was here that Wolfgang accomplished his celebrated feat of musical ear and memory. It was the custom on Wednesday and Friday in Holy Week for the choir of the Pope's household to sing the Miserere (Ps. 50) composed by Dom. Allegri, which was arranged alternately for a four and five part chorus, having a final chorus in nine parts. This performance was universally considered as one of the most wonderful in Rome; the impression made by it, in conjunction with the solemn rites it accompanied, was always described as overpowering. 'You know,' writes L. Mozart, 'that this celebrated Miserere is so jealously guarded, that members of the chapel are forbidden, under pain of excommunication, to take their parts out of the chapel, or to copy, or allow it to be copied. We have got it, notwithstanding. Wolfgang has written it down, and I should have sent it to Salzburg in this letter were not our presence necessary for its production. More depends on the performance than even on the composition. Besides, we must not let our secret fall into other hands, *ut non incurramus, mediate vel immediate, in censuram ecclesiæ.*' When the performance was repeated on Good Friday, Wolfgang took the manuscript with him into the chapel, and holding it in his hat, corrected some passages where his memory had not been quite true. The affair became known, and naturally made a great

sensation; Wolfgang was called upon to execute the Miserere in presence of the Papal singer, Christofori, who was amazed at its correctness. L. Mozart's news excited consternation in Salzburg, mother and daughter believing that Wolfgang had sinned in transcribing the Miserere, and fearing unpleasant consequences if it should become known. 'When we read your ideas about the Miserere,' answered the father, 'we both laughed loud and long. You need not be in the least afraid. It is taken in quite another way. All Rome and the Pope himself know that Wolfgang has written the Miserere, and instead of punishment, it has brought him honour. You must not fail to show my letter everywhere, and let His Grace the Archbishop know of it." This feat was undoubtedly a remarkable one, but all Mozart's biographers have borne witness to the fact that he possessed an ear of wonderful delicacy and retentive power. Jahn states that when Mozart was not more than five years old he observed that his own violin was tuned an eighth of a tone higher than one belonging to Herr Schachtner, a friend of his father's, upon which he had played a day or two previous, and on comparison this proved to be the case.

121. Another great composer who, like Mozart, possessed a phenomenal power of memory was MENDELSSOHN. He, also, during a visit to Rome, performed the feat of recording Allegri's Miserere, whilst the following story, the particulars of which have been supplied to me by Mr. T. L. Southgate, describes a feat of a somewhat similar nature. Mendelssohn, when in England, was sometimes the guest of Attwood, the organist of St. Paul's Cathedral. During one of his visits he heard at the Cathedral a composition, either a Service or an Anthem of Attwood's. This pleased him so much that he offered to score it for the orchestra. Attwood readily accepted Mendelssohn's offer, but the matter was not again referred to until after Mendelssohn's return to Germany, when Attwood wrote to him offering to send a copy of the work in question for reference. Mendelssohn's reply was a full orchestral score of it, which he had completed from memory, after hearing it once or perhaps twice at St. Paul's. A comparison of this full score with Attwood's vocal score showed that in no respect had his memory failed him.

122. That Mendelssohn was an earnest student of all Bach's works is well known, and his great admiration of the St. Matthew "Passion" led him to revive that work at Berlin in 1829, the centenary year of its first production. Referring to this event, the following passage, taken from some anecdotes of Mendelssohn by Pastor Julius Schubring, of which a translation appeared in the *Musical World* of May 12th and 19th, 1866, is worth recalling. The writer says, "How thoroughly he (Mendelssohn) had rendered himself master of this work was proved by his directing one of the later rehearsals at the piano without any music before him, and by his remarking, at the conclusion of the movement, 'In the twenty-third bar the soprano has C and not C sharp;'" whilst Sir Charles Hallé in his Autobiography gives us an account of what happened at the performance of this same piece. He says, "It is well-known that when he (Mendelssohn) revived Bach's 'Passion Music,' and conducted the first performance of that immortal work, after it had been dormant for

about a century, he found, stepping to the conductor's desk, that a score, similar in binding and thickness, but of another work, had been brought by mistake. He conducted this amazingly complicated work by heart, turning leaf after leaf of the book he had before him, in order not to create any feeling of uneasiness on the part of the executants." Another story, which bears witness to the wonderful accuracy with which he knew the scores of works he studied, is related by Ferdinand Hiller in his "Mendelssohn." At a weekly musical gathering at the Abbé Bardin's, when both Hiller and Mendelssohn were present, Hiller writes, "I had just been playing Beethoven's E flat Concerto in public, and they asked for it again on one of these afternoons. The parts were all there, and the string quartet too, but no players for the wind. 'I will do the wind,' said Mendelssohn, and sitting down to a small piano which stood near the grand one, he filled in the wind parts from memory so completely, that I don't believe even a note of the second horn was wanting, and all as simply and naturally done as if it were nothing."

123. All the above, however, are quite eclipsed by the following, which is recorded by Max Müller in his "Auld Lang Syne," and took place on the occasion of Liszt's first appearance in Leipzig. "Mendelssohn," says the writer, "gave a matinée musicale at his house, all the best known musicians of the place being present. I remember, though vaguely, David, Kalliwoda, Hiller; I doubt whether Schumann and Clara Wieck were present. Well, Liszt appeared in his Hungarian costume, wild and magnificent. He told Mendelssohn that he had written something special for him. He sat down, and swaying right and left on his music stool, played a Hungarian melody, and then three or four variations, one more incredible than the other. We st_od amazed, and after everybody had paid his compliments to the hero of the day, some of Mendelssohn's friends gathered round him and said, 'Ah, Felix, now we can pack up. No one can do that; it is over with us!' Mendelssohn smiled; and when Liszt came up to him, asking him to play something in turn he laughed and said that he never played now; and this to a certain extent was true. He did not give much time to practising then, but worked chiefly at composing and directing his concerts. However, Liszt would take no refusal, and so at last little Mendelssohn with his own charming playfulness said, 'Well, I'll play, but you must promise me not to be angry.' And what did he play? He sat down and played first of all Liszt's Hungarian melody, and then one variation after another, so that none but Liszt himself could have told the difference. We all trembled lest Liszt should be offended, for Mendelssohn could not keep himself from slightly imitating Liszt's movements and raptures. However, Mendelssohn managed never to offend man, woman, or child; Liszt laughed, applauded, and admitted that 'no one, not he himself, could have performed such a bravura." How far Mendelssohn's powers of execution would meet the demands of a piece written by Liszt, probably with the express object of displaying his own marvellous powers upon an occasion of exceptional importance, must remain an unanswered question, but after making allowance for large deficiences, this feat is perhaps the most wonderful of its kind on record.

124. One of a similar although less exacting nature was performed by FERDINAND HILLER, and has been communicated to me by Mr. C. Ainslie Barry, who at one time was a pupil of Hiller's at the Cologne Conservatoire. During a composition lesson Hiller left the class room and went for some time into an adjoining room. In his absence Mr. Barry's fellow pupil played over an unfinished Scherzo for the piano which he had brought to show his master. Hiller having heard the performance whilst in the adjoining room, on his return, inquired why it was left unfinished, and then sat down at the piano, played the Scherzo from memory, added a Trio and repeated the Scherzo, finishing it off with a coda.

125. HANS VON BÜLOW has always been famous for his remarkable powers of memory. Mr. Dannreuther, in his article on Bülow in Sir George Grove's "Dictionary of Music and Musicians," says, "It would be difficult to mention a work of any importance by any composer for the piano, which he has not played in public and by heart. His prodigious musical memory has enabled him also as a conductor to perform feats which have never before been attempted, and will in all likelihood not be imitated." The fashion of conducting from memory was introduced by Bülow, and his wonderfully accurate knowledge of orchestral scores was undoubtedly remarkable. It is said of him that at the rehearsal for a concert in London, at the conclusion of the performance of a movement from one of Beethoven's Symphonies which he was conducting from memory, after a few moments' calculation he informed one of the second wind players that at a certain bar, so many bars from the end, he had played a wrong note, at the same time informing the offender what he had played and what he ought to have played. But perhaps Bülow's most prodigious feat in this direction was the conducting from memory of the first performance of Wagner's "Tristan and Isolde" at Munich, in 1865. Only those who know the complexity of a Wagner Opera, and the intricate nature of the score, can fully appreciate such a performance.

126. The piano recitals which Bulow gave in London at different times bore ample witness to his prodigious memory for piano music, the occasion when he played the five latest Sonatas of Beethoven being one of the most remarkable. The following story of a feat of memory by him, for the details of which I am indebted to Miss Constance Bache, is interesting as showing the wonderful reliability of his memory under quite exceptional conditions. Miss Bache writes as follows:—
"A number of versions are given of the following story, which Bülow could never hear without bursting with laughter. The following is his own version:—I once played a piece in public for the first time, which I learned from the notes. This seems impossible, yet for once it is true. A friend of mine had put down a piece of his own in my next concert, and I had not the time even to play it through. I therefore took the copy with me in the train, studied it in the carriage, and played it in the evening." Miss Bache continues:—"I believe it was at Riga, or some other place on the Baltic Sea, and that the account first appeared in the local newspaper."

127. Whilst we are considering the special subject of playing piano-

music from memory, it may not be uninteresting to make a slight digression into some of the by-paths of musical criticism of past years and see how those who guided public opinion, regarded memory playing when it was the exception rather than the rule. In the year 1861, the late SIR (then Mr.) CHARLES HALLÉ gave a series of Beethoven Recitals at St. James's Hall, when he played the whole of the piano Sonatas. After the first "recital," which included the first four Sonatas, the following notice, from the pen of the late Mr. J. W. Davison, appeared in "The Times" of May 20th, and shows that his playing them from memory was looked upon in no favourable light. "Mr. Charles Hallé," says the *Times*' critic, "has undertaken a no less arduous than honourable task. A good many pianists (virtuosi included) would be somewhat at a loss to play any one of the Sonatas of Beethoven, even with the music to refer to at convenience; but Mr. Hallé proposes to essay them all in a series of eight concerts—we beg pardon, 'recitals'—and if the performance of Friday may be regarded as a precedent, all *without book*. However doubtful the wisdom of such a risk, it is impossible not to admire the artistic self-reliance that suggested it. No less than 35 Sonatas for the pianoforte alone are published under the name of Beethoven; and supposing, as is most likely to be the case, the three early ones, which—though printed 13 years before the set of trios dedicated to Prince Lichnowski (Op. 1)—Beethoven himself repudiated, and the two Sonatinas (Op. 49) omitted from the scheme, Mr. Hallé will still have 30 Sonatas, for the most part works of a large calibre, to commit (or re-commit, for possibly in earlier days the feat may have been already accomplished) to memory! The tenth labour of a musical Hercules would scarcely amount to more." After a criticism of the performance the writer continues:—"All these four Sonatas, as we have hinted, were given with no other index than that of memory to aid the performer. The entirely successful result proved that in this instance he required no other; but we confess we shall not be sorry if at the next 'recital,' when the Three Sonatas, Op. 10, and No. 1, of Op. 14, are to be performed, we obtain a glimpse of the printed music on the desk of the pianoforte. *Il ne faut pas tenter les dieux.*"

128. That the *Times*' critic did not get that ardently desired glimpse of the printed music may be gathered from his second notice of the same series of recitals, which appeared on June 3rd, and runs as follows:—"Mr. Charles Hallé is progressing triumphantly with the exceptional task he has set himself—that of performing in immediate succession the whole of Beethoven's pianoforte Sonatas. Since we last alluded to the subject he has played the three Sonatas, Op. 10, the Sonata Patetica, and the two Sonatas Op. 14, the Sonata in B flat Op. 22, and the Sonata in A flat Op. 26, (with the well-known Variations and Funeral march)—all as before without the advantage of the music to refer to. On this last point, while according to Mr. Hallé the credit due to an exertion of the faculty of retention almost unprecedented—we are by no means inclined to retract what was said in allusion to his first recital. When he appears at the instrument even his warmest admirers and most enthusiastic panegyrists can hardly feel otherwise than apprehensive; while mere impartial hearers who may happen to know the Sonatas almost

as intimately as Mr. Hallé himself (without be it understood, the singular ability which enables him to execute them, more or less perfectly, from memory) are, perhaps, in the end less thoroughly satisfied than they might be if the accomplished German pianist had set to work *con amore* without a thought of self display, to interpret Beethoven—as few like himself are able to interpret him—for Beethoven's sake alone. Nevertheless, having successfully gone through twelve Sonatas without book, Mr. Hallé, it may be fairly argued, is justified in proceeding as he has begun." After this second notice, we are told the recitalist gave way and placed the book before him on the desk, although he still continued to play from memory.

129. The fashion of pianoforte "recitals" set by Mr. Hallé in 1861 evidently came to stay, despite the strictures of the most eminent musical critics of the day in the most powerful periodicals "The Times" and "The Athenæum," and when, in 1873, BÜLOW paid us a visit, and surprised the musical world with his wonderful powers of execution and memory, we find the latter paper chronicles his performance with awe and wonder, but still not with unmixed admiration. The writer says, "He (Bulow) had no music before his eyes to guide him, he confided in his memory and it never faltered ; it was a prodigious effort, almost inconceivable, and perhaps somewhat too daring and hazardous."

130. We cannot draw this digression to a close without mentioning the remarkable series of seven historical pianoforte recitals which were given in London by RUBINSTEIN in 1886. It may be interesting to revive some of the programmes, in order to give an idea of the feat performed by this prince of pianists. The Beethoven one comprised eight Sonatas. Op. 27 in C sharp minor; Op. 31, No. 2, in D minor; Op. 53 ("Waldstein"); Op. 57 ("Appassionata"); Op. 90, in E minor; Op. 101 in A major; Op. 109 in E major; Op. 111 in C minor. The Chopin recital included the Fantasia in F minor, six Preludes, four Mazurkas, two Impromptus, three Nocturnes, four Ballades, three Polonaises, the Sonata in B flat minor and other items ; and the Schumann, the Fantasia in C, Kreisleriana, Etudes Symphoniques, Sonata in F sharp, four numbers of the Phantasiestück, "Vogels als Prophet," Romance in D minor and the Carnival. On this occasion the Press marvelled but it did not protest. It must be conceded that in the present day the ability to play from memory must be possessed by every pianist who would gain public favour, and although both musicians and musical critics regard the prevailing fashion as one of not unmixed good they are unable to influence public opinion to any effectual degree.

131. Returning now to our original theme, which is the recording of memory performances, and not the reviving of musical criticisms, we stated above that the fashion of conducting from memory was set by Bülow, and amongst living conductors who have sustained the tradition, DR. HANS RICHTER is perhaps the most prominent. His method of conducting without the book is known to every one who has attended a Richter concert, but the degree to which he is conversant with absolutely every detail of a score is perhaps only appreciated by the privileged few who gain admission to his orchestral

rehearsals. These, like his performances, are conducted from memory, and the least inaccuracy either as to notes, rhythm or phrasing, no matter how subordinate the part, or how complex the score, is instantly detected by him, and in order to set the player right he may either sing the passage, or even show upon the instrument how it should be played, if such were necessary. In 1876 he directed the whole of the rehearsals and performances of Wagner's "Ring" at Bayreuth, and it was said, at the conclusion of the Festival, that if the whole of the scores had been lost, Dr. Richter could have written them out from memory, a feat which every student of Wagner would know to be absolutely phenomenal.

132. The late Professor of Music at Oxford, the REV. SIR FREDERICK GORE OUSELEY, was always remarkable for his general power of musical memory as well as for his exceptional power of retaining definite pitches. The Rev. J. Hampton, Warden of St. Michael's College, Tenbury, has contributed the following passage, illustrative of these gifts, to Mr. Havergal's Memorials of Sir Frederick:—"At Cambridge, in the year 1861, I heard Beethoven's Septett for the first time, and on my return mentioned the fact to Sir Frederick, who immediately went to the piano and commenced the work, pointing out each instrument that had any prominent part. He played on for 20 minutes and then only stopped from fatigue. I told him, that I wondered that I had never heard him play it before. He said that he had never done so—had not seen it in print, and only heard it once in his life, ten years before in Rome. When living in London it was his delight to visit the organ lofts of St. Paul's and Westminster Abbey. After an absence of several months in Spain, Italy, Germany, Switzerland, and Paris, where he had tried every organ of any size, he returned to England and soon visited his friend Sir John Goss at St. Paul's. Sir John asked him to sound C, which he did, and then Sir John put down B, which was in perfect tune, whereupon Sir Frederick immediately smiled and said, 'You have had all the pipes cut down since I was last here.' Sir John assured me that the pitch of the organ *had* been raised a semitone."

133. The following, which is supplied by Mr. T. L. Southgate to Sir Frederick's "Life," is also worth quoting as evidence of the possession of an exceptional retentive power. Mr. Southgate says, "We were discussing the question of dancing as a part of Church public worship, and I read him a letter received from a friend in Abyssinia who told me that there they still 'danced before the Lord,' as it is recorded David did. 'Oh,' said Ouseley with a smile, 'I have seen that much nearer home. In 1851 I went to Spain for a tour, and on a special high day I saw a solemn *fandango* danced in front of the high altar at Seville; and this was the music it was danced to.' He then went to the piano and played a delicate little piece, quite Spanish in tone, with the exception of a peculiar use of the chord of the 'Italian Sixth.' I asked him whether that was correct, and expressed astonishment that he should have remembered this piece, heard but once some thirty-six years ago. 'Quite right,' he replied, 'I thought that chord would startle you,' and then he continued, 'If I thoroughly give my mind to receive a piece of music, I generally succeed in mastering it, and never afterwards forget it.'"

134. Amongst English musicians who are living, and who are known to possess exceptional powers of memory, SIR WALTER PARRATT, Private Organist to the Queen, stands pre-eminent. Sir Walter's memory was evidently developed quite early, for Sir George Grove, in his Dictionary, relates the fact that "at the age of 10 he played on one occasion the whole of the 48 preludes and fugues of Bach by heart without notice." Another exceptional exercise of his wonderful power took place whilst he was organist of St. Paul's Church, Huddersfield. At a competition for a vacant post in the choir, an applicant possessed only one copy of the solo he wished to sing. As he was unable to sing it without the assistance of the printed copy, and it was necessary for him, whilst singing it, to stand in the choir stalls and quite away from the organ, he was on the horns of a dilemma until Sir Walter, then a youth of about 12 or 13, came to his rescue, and after glancing at the music for a moment, accompanied it from memory. In addition to his brilliant gifts as a musician, Sir Walter is a fine chess player, and during a visit to the late Sir Frederick Ouseley at Tenbury, he performed a feat which, like the one recorded of Mendelssohn in par. 123, probably stands alone amongst memory performances. The Rev. J. Hampton, who succeeded the late Sir Frederick Ouseley as Warden of St. Michael's College, Tenbury, was present on the occasion, and has kindly supplied me with the following description of what took place. His narrative runs as follows:—"In one of the lodgings attached to St. Michael's College, Tenbury, some eight or ten men were assembled. Von Holst and Sir Walter played on the piano in turn such music as was asked for, and always from memory. This went on for some time, when the chess board was brought out, and Sir Walter proposed to play two men in consultation while he remained at the piano, still playing anything asked for, either from Bach, Mozart, Beethoven, Mendelssohn or Chopin. He never looked at the chess board, but continued to converse with those around, who did all they could to distract him, although without success. His memory never failed him for at least an hour, when the game was won by him, and he told us how he had been watching the chances of a poor fly which had become entangled in a spider's web. Both the antagonists come here occasionally, and have often spoken of the memorable occasion."

135. We have come to the end of our records, but in them we seem to have touched but the fringe of a deeply interesting subject, and one which could supply many more pages of interesting reading. Such incidents are often known only to private friends and pupils, and the details rarely made public. We should, therefore, be grateful to any of our readers, who, knowing the particulars of any exceptional and uncommon memory performances in connection with music, which it would be interesting to permanently record, would communicate with us, with a view to the insertion of the particulars of such performances in a subsequent issue of this work.

INDEX TO MUSICAL EXAMPLES AND REFERENCES.

Where no Example number is given, a passage from the work is simply referred to in the text.

BEETHOVEN.

EXAMPLE.				PAR.
	Sonata, Op. 2, No. 1	...	...	104
	,, Op. 2, No. 2	...	...	50
16	,, Op. 2, No. 3	...	...	40
19	,, Op. 2, No. 3	...	..	43
27	,, Op. 2, No. 3	...	...	55-6
28	,, Op. 2, No. 3	...	...	55-6
21	,, Op. 10, No. 1	...	...	47
14	,, Op. 14, No. 2	...	...	34
	,, Op. 22	...	...	49
	,, Op. 26	...	...	27
	,, Op. 31, No. 1	...	...	49
	,, Op. 31, No. 2	...	...	7
	,, Op. 31, No. 2	...	...	49
	,, Op. 31, No. 3	...	...	50
1	,, Op. 53	...	...	7
	,, Op. 57	...	...	49
31	,, Op. 57	...	...	56
	,, Op. 110	...	...	50

BRAHMS.

| 22 | Rhapsody, Op. 79, No. 1 ... | 47, 110 |

CHOPIN.

8	Sonata, Op. 4	...	...	...	29
26	Scherzo, Op. 20	...	...	...	53
4	Ballade, Op. 23	...	...	...	24
13	Etude, Op. 25, No. 2	...	...	32
17	Prelude, Op. 28, No. 19 ...	...	43

EXAMPLE.				PAR.
15	Scherzo, Op. 31	...	...	...	38
23	,, Op. 31	...	...	...	50
6	Ballade, Op. 47	...	...	26, 39, 62
12	,, Op. 52	...	...	31-38
	Fantaisie-Impromptu, Op. 66	...	34

MENDELSSOHN.

5	Capriccio, Op. 5	...	...	...	25
7	Rondo Capriccio, Op. 14	...	...	27
9	Concerto, Op. 25	...	...	...	29
10	Phantasie, Op. 28	...	...	...	29
11	,, Op. 28	...	...	30, 110
18	Variations Serieuses, Op. 54	...	43

SCHUBERT.

| 30 | Fantaisie, Op. 15 | ... | .— | ... | 56 |

SCHUMANN.

32	Intermezzi, Op. 4, No. 2	...	...	56
20	"Aufschwung," Op. 12	...	...	47
	"Grillen," Op. 12	...	..	...	47
24	Sonata, Op. 22	...	...	...	52
25	,, Op. 22	...	...	...	52

WEBER.

2	Sonata, Op. 39	...	...	...	24
3	,, Op. 39	...	...	...	24
29	,, Op. 39	...	...	...	55

GENERAL INDEX.

The numbers in all cases refer to the Paragraphs *not to the pages.*

	PAR.
ABSOLUTE PITCH, Sense of	13
BACH, St. Matthew, "Passion," and Mendelssohn...	122
Beethoven, Analysis of 1st Movement of Sonata, Op. 2, No. 1 ...	104
———— "Devices"	7
———— "Methods"	48, 105
Bülow, Hans von, the memory of	125, 129
COMPARISON of the styles of different composers	98, 99
Concertos, memorization of	108
Concentration, continuous ...	42, 87, 96
———— motives to	84
Conditions favourable to memorizing	79 et seq.
EAR-TESTS in Examinations	114
Ear-training	8, 12, 71, 114
Elaboration, Form and Progression of	54
———— of a single chord	52
———— of a progression of chords ...	53
Examinations, Ear-tests in	114
———— influence of	111
———— memory performance in ...	118
FINGER MEMORY	23
HALLÉ, Sir Charles, introduction of "Recitals" by	127
Harmonic basis of passages	51
Harmony, advantage of a knowledge of	28, 45
———— examinations and ear-tests ...	114
———— right and wrong methods of study	74
Hiller, Ferdinand, Memory performance of	124

	PAR.
INTELLECTUAL TENDENCIES, to what due	67
"LAW OF CONTIGUITY"	18
Listening, Intelligent	6
Liszt and Mendelssohn	123
MEMORY, GENERAL	1
———— INTELLECTUAL ...	44 et seq.
———— ———— upon what its employment depends	57
———— MUSCULAR	18 et seq.
———— ———— automatic employment	19, 34
———— ———— its connection with Visual Memory...	39
———— ———— suitable passages	23
———— ———— suitable and unsuitable, passages compared...	32, 33
———— MUSICAL	5 et seq.
———— ———— growth of	8
———— ———— perfect form of	13
———— ———— possibilities of	15
———— ———— upon what its value depends	11
———— PERFORMANCES ...	119 et seq.
———— ———— criticisms of	127
———— ———— evils of	77
———— ———— favourable conditions ...	81
———— ———— in Examinations	118
———— ———— powers employed	15
———— ———— rehearsing for ...	109, 110
———— ———— selection of pieces... ...	93
———— ———— value of	75, 76
———— ———— value of early training ...	92
———— ———— when may be introduced ...	91
———— ———— with Orchestra	108
———— SPECIAL, Forms of ...	1 et seq.
———— ———— law as to employment of in Piano playing	68
———— ———— natural power of	83

PAR.

MEMORY, SPECIAL—
———— relative degree possessed
      by different senses ... 66
———— VISUAL ... . 35 *et seq.*
———— ——— and Muscular Memory ... 39
———— ——— and Visual Control 31, 42
Method of Study 47 *et seq.;* 63, 80, 102 *et seq.*
Mendelssohn, Feats of Memory 121 *et seq.*
Mental Rehearsal 110
Mozart, his remarkable ear ... 13, 120
———— his retentive Memory ... 120
Music, material of 12
———— nature of 61
Musical Critics and Memory Performances ... ... 127 *et seq.*
MUSICAL EDUCATION, a neglected branch of ... ... 71 *et seq.*
———— controlled by Examinations 111 *et seq.*
———— what it should include ... 12, 76
Musical Form, how it appeals to the Memory 6, 7
———— its study an aid to memory playing 47

NATURAL TASTES, to what due ... 3, 4

OUSELEY, Sir Frederick, the memory of 132

PARRATT, Sir Walter, the memory of 133
PASSAGES, Form of ... ...
———— brilliant 23
———— broken chord 27, 55
———— chordal 40
———— chords in different positions ... 43
———— evolved from a single chord 52
———— evolved from a progression ... 53
———— extended 43
———— grand arpeggios 26
———— harmonic basis of 51
———— irregular 31

PAR.

PASSAGES—
———— scale extended 24
———— short scale 25
———— which differ in details 30, 103
———— which differ in their progress 47
———— which include wide skips ... 43
———— which require the hands to be crossed 43
———— which present special difficulties 63
———— with recurring figures 29, 38, 55 *et seq.*
———— with a regular progression in the bass 49
———— with a regular sequence of keys 50
———— with repetitions of a tonal sequence 50
Playing by Ear 12
Peculiarities of Individuals 65
Piano Playing, an evil result of ... 73
———— complexity of operation ... 15
———— early difficulties 37
———— from Memory 75
———— upon what proficiency depends 4, 21

READING MUSIC ... ... 72 *et seq.*
Reflex movements 19
Rehearsing away from Piano 110
———— from Memory 109
Repetition, extent necessary 88
Richter, Dr. Hans, the memory of ... 131
Rubenstein, Historical recitals ... 130

SUPERIOR FACULTIES, the influence of 3, 67

TECHNIQUE and Muscular Memory ... 20

VISUAL CONTROL ... 31, 42 *et seq.*
———— Memory ... ... 35 *et seq.*

	RIEMANN, Dr. H.—*(Contd.)*		
	Analysis of J. S. Bach's "48 Preludes and Fugues."		
9205	Part I. 24 Preludes and Fugues. Fourth Impression ... ...Bound	2	-
9206	Part II. 24 Preludes and Fugues. Third Impression ... ...Bound	2	-
	ROCKSTRO, W. S. Practical Harmony. ...Bound	2	-
	Key to "Practical Harmony"	1	6
	Rules of Counterpoint ... ...Bound	2	-
	A History of Music. Twenty-fifth Edition. Bound	2	-
9193	**RUBINSTEIN, A.** Music and its Masters. A Conversation. Second Impression ... ...Bound	2	-
9212	**SCHROEDER, C.** Handbook of Violin and Viola Playing. Fourth Impression ... ...Bound	2	-
9212a	Guide through Violin and Viola Literature. Third Impression ... ... Bound 6d. Paper	-	4
9211	Catechism of Violoncello Playing. Third Impr. Bound	2	-
9213	Handbook of Conducting. (J. Matthews.) Fourth Impression ... ...Bound	2	-
9194	**SCHUMANN.** Advice to Young Musicians	-	6
10146	**SHEDLOCK, J. S.** Beethoven's Pianoforte Sonatas. The Origin and Respective Values of Various Readings	1	-
10148	**SHINN, DR. F. G.** Elementary Ear-Training. I. Melodic		
10149	II. Harmonic and Contrapuntal		
	A Method of Teaching Harmony based upon Ear-Training:		
10150	I. Diatonic Harmony		
10151	II. Chromatic Harmony and Exceptional Progression		
10152	Musical Memory and its Cultivation...		
10121	**SIBLEY, C.** The Voice and its Control	1	-
10131	**SIMPSON, J.** 300 Questions on the Grammar of Music. Based on the Syllabus of the Associated Board of the R.A.M. and R.C.M.	1	-
10132	Key to the above	1	-
10133	400 Questions on the Rudiments of Music	1	6
10134	Key to the above	1	6
10135	A concise textbook on the Rudiments of Music ...	1	6
9196	**STIELER, J.** The Great German Composers. Biographical Notices, with some account of their Works. Illustrated ... ...Bound	3	6
	SUTTON, R. Elements of the Theory of Music. Bound	2	-
10109	**WARREN, J.** Catechism of the Harmonium ...	-	6
	WEST, G. F. Hints to Young Teachers of the Pianoforte	1	-
	WHITTINGHAM, A. 200 Questions and Exercises on F. Davenport's "Elements of Music"... ...	-	6

AUGENER Ltd.
63 CONDUIT STREET (Regent Street Corner),
57 HIGH STREET, MARYLEBONE & 18 GREAT MARLBOROUGH STREET,
LONDON, W. 1.

www.ingramcontent.com/pod-product-compliance
Lightning Source LLC
Chambersburg PA
CBHW031608110426
42742CB00037B/1334